BARN DOORS

when God swings them wide

BARN DOORS

when God swings them wide

EMMA BROCH STUART

WhiteFire Publishing

BARN DOORS: WHEN GOD SWINGS THEM WIDE

Copyright © 2017, Emma Broch Stuart

All rights reserved. Reproduction in part or in whole is strictly forbidden without the express written consent of the publisher.

WhiteFire Publishing
13607 Bedford Rd NE
Cumberland, MD 21502

ISBN: 978-1-946531-00-1 (print)
978-1-939023-91-9 (digital)

All Scripture quotations, unless otherwise indicated, are taken from the Holy Bible, New International Version®, NIV®. Copyright ©1973, 1978, 1984, 2011 by Biblica, Inc.™ Used by permission of Zondervan. All rights reserved worldwide. www.zondervan.com The "NIV" and "New International Version" are trademarks registered in the United States Patent and Trademark Office by Biblica, Inc.™

Scripture quotations noted NKJV are taken from the New King James Version®. Copyright © 1982 by Thomas Nelson. Used by permission. All rights reserved.

Scripture quotations noted NASB are taken from the New American Standard Bible® (NASB), Copyright © 1960, 1962, 1963, 1968, 1971, 1972, 1973, 1975, 1977, 1995 by The Lockman Foundation Used by permission. www.Lockman.org.

Scripture quotations noted NLT are are taken from the Holy Bible, New Living Translation, copyright ©1996, 2004, 2007, 2013, 2015 by Tyndale House Foundation. Used by permission of Tyndale House Publishers, Inc., Carol Stream, Illinois 60188. All rights reserved.

I will give thanks to you, Lord, with all my heart;
I will tell of all your wonderful deeds.
~ Psalm 9:1

Table of Contents

Barn Doors and Neon Lights / 11

Love Stains / 13

Third Verse / 17

Stickers in the Sky / 20

Bald Tooth Fairy / 23

Candy Is a Love Language / 26

Grace and Law Collide / 31

Birthday Buddy / 35

Friendship Tree / 38

All God's Creatures / 41

Snarky Tension / 45

Sock Ministry / 49

From Paris to Potholes / 52

Cake Crumbs and Sequins / 56

I Find Peace / 59

Peace Finds Me / 65

Mountain Transforms to Monster / 68

The Purple Monster / 71

Love Lines / 73

Circle of Prayer / 77

Our Heart's Closet / 80

Pockets of Greatness / 83

Humanity Has a Name / 88

Just Past the City Limits / 93

Different Streets / 96

The Ark of Waiting / 99

Homeless for a Day / 104

Bathroom Buddies / 107

Bullets of Profoundness / 110

In Between / 115

Bridge Between Two Camps / 116

The Attitude Jar / 119

Connecting at the Well / 121

Little Dips in the Well / 126

♡ Thinking / 131

Ruth in the Season / 133

Morning into Dancing / 135

Fill in the Blanks / 138

Names of God / 145

Circle Around the Block / 149

Bank of the Jordan / 152

Garments of Readiness / 155

The Jesus House / 158

Deep Calls to Deep / 161

Radical Hospitality / 165

Used for Mighty Things / 167

When Our Colors Line Up and Fly / 170

Ribbons and Bows / 172

Gifts Piled High / 176

The Gift of all Things / 179

The Gift of Time / 182

The Gift of Breath / 186

The Gift of Authority / 188

The Gift of Ownership / 192

The Gift of Surrender / 196

The Gift of Perspective / 202

The Gift of Joy in All Circumstances / 207

The Gift of Forgiveness / 211

The Gift of Dependency / 214

The Gift of Ships / 217

Closing Doors / 221

Love You / 223

Notes / 225

Barn Doors and Neon Lights

It wasn't so long ago that I turned my life over to God. During the last ten years, He's proven to be better equipped than I at leading—and showing me that I was created to follow. For some people, that moment of relinquishing control is like throwing God the car keys and jumping in the passenger seat and letting Him drive. For me, it was more like turning the machete over to God so He could hack through a past made up of thick jungle vines, suffocating vegetation, and a maze of gnarled tree roots. Over time, the jungle chaos that was my life transformed into a path of righteousness where fruit and flower blossoms replaced tangled roots and branches of thorns. I have followed behind for ten years, humbled by the beauty that springs up before my eyes.

Those blossoms only scent my path through a lifestyle of seeking God's will and enjoying the peace that comes from a harvest of obedience and gratitude. *Barn Doors* uncovers the beauty springing up before my eyes as I journey with Him. Rusty hinges creak as God swings *Barn Doors* wide and invites you to join Him and me at the table. A table spread with a decade of bounty—beautiful gifts,

Barn Doors

astounding joy, pure goodness, and overflowing love. I have reaped a harvest of obedience and deep gratitude, not to keep for myself but to share with all of you.

As I walk with Him, knowing His clear direction for my life isn't always easy. Sometimes He gives me a blank canvas and lets me paint to my heart's content—as long as I stay within the boundaries of the canvas. When I feel Him leading me down a certain road, I immediately ask for confirmation. And not subtle confirmation. Not a whisper on a breeze. No, I need barn doors to swing wide open and neon lights to flash "This way! This way!" That is my confirmation style. I desire more than anything to be obediently in His will at all times.

God delights in pulling open those creaking doors and plugging in the lights that guide me down the right path. As my spiritual roots grow, He doesn't always open those barn doors as wide, nor does He always plug in the neon. But He never fails to confirm no matter how many times I ask. He delights in showing me His goodness. And He delights in me when my spiritual eyes can spot His confirmation no matter how it arrives, whether flashing and stampeding through a wide-open door or fluttering on a butterfly wing.

Barn Doors is a collection of those butterfly wings fluttering on breezes, a harvest of God's goodness in my life, and rusty hinges on barn doors that creak when God swings them wide.

Love Stains

Love does a lot of things, but we don't usually associate love with stains. I have three lovely examples of when love stains. Groups of three are a delight to me, since I have three children. As luck would have it, my three examples are about each of them. They have been little love stains in action!

In 2012, ten months before returning to the states, my daughter and I moved in with a friend as a way to save money and purge our belongings. The first purge was easy because not much fit into our attic bedroom with its low ceilings and steep flight of stairs. This love stain didn't happen in the attic, so we'll have to go down those steep stairs and wander into the unusually narrow hallway between the toilet room and the bathroom. There was no wiggle room in that hallway.

My daughter (whose middle name is Emma—get it? Emma Broch Stuart) bonded instantly with my French friend. She was glued to her side almost every moment from the time school let out until bedtime. After a few months, my friend noticed that every time I spoke to my daughter, I used a different pet name—sometimes more than one in a short conversation. Established pet names blended in

Barn Doors

with made-in-the-moment pet names. My daughter had gotten so used to it, she didn't even notice. But my friend did, and I told her I didn't know why pet names flowed naturally as I conversed with her. Names like Baby Flower, Little Love, Pork Chop, Sweetness, Lovebug, and Buttercup. Even names from books we read together like Petunia May—who was a dreamer—and Daisy Dawson, a dawdler. Every time my daughter dawdled, I called her Daisy Dawson.

A few weeks went by, and my friend was hugging Little Love in the kitchen one day, asking her about school. As they conversed in French, several pet names were spoken over my Baby Flower. Names like Ma Puce, Mon Cœur, Chèrie. Even made-in-the-moment names like Chouchou and Woogie. Suddenly my friend gasped. "I see what you mean! Calling her pet names just comes out of your mouth."

That love stain didn't happen in the kitchen, I know, but you have to pass through the kitchen to get to the hallway where it did happen. Sweetness saw my friend coming out of the bathroom one day and ran to her in the doorway of the narrow hall and threw her little Buttercup arms around her, sloshing my friend's coffee so that it spilled down the wall. My Petunia May did not get burned; the wallpaper soaked the coffee right up. And left the biggest stain. Pork Chop felt really bad for making my friend spill her coffee, but my friend shrugged it off and squealed, "Woogie, your love stains!"

And so it does. Goodness, she makes me smile.

My oldest son (whose middle name is Broch—where the Broch in my writing name comes from) had a couple of close French friends who came to his fourteenth birthday party. His birthday is in December, but we celebrated it during the summer with an outdoor BBQ. I pulled his two close friends aside and conned them into picking up my son's birthday cake and throwing it in his face. I didn't waste sugar on this cake, or frosting; cheap whipped topping covered it instead. The plan was to stand on either side of him and wait until we sang "Happy Birthday"; after, I would pull out the candles so those didn't get jabbed into an eye, and then they were to go for it! There my son sat, grinning with that teenager grin of his while we sang. As soon as he blew out the candles, the two friends stuck their hands into the sides of the cake and paused. They both realized they'd forgotten to wait for me to take out the candles. That teenager grin changed to a scowl. Why on earth he didn't run, I'll never know. But his friends kept their hands in the cake while the candles were removed with my son scowling back and forth at the two of them. How dare they touch his cake. He never understood their intent until it was smashed in his face.

That was one of my favorite days of love staining ever! The funniest moment was his brother howling at the other end of the table because the cake was ruined. At eight years old, he was not a good secret keeper, so he was never let in on the plan. We fetched the real cake from the fridge but not before my son chased everyone down and stained them with fake cake and fake frosting.

That howling little brother hated stains. Of any kind. This son is represented by the name Stuart in my writing name and therefore comes at the end of my love staining chapter. When he was two, he would eat oatmeal like this: take a bite, stiffen up, and squeal until I wiped the tiniest hint of oatmeal from his mouth. He would chew, swallow, and start the process all over again. His best two-year-old friend was a heathen. There's no other way to describe her, bless her little heathen heart. She'd sit at that plastic picnic table and watch her friend go berserk over a speck of oatmeal stuck to his chin. She'd let him do this a few times before picking up her bowl of runny oatmeal and turning it upside down over her head.

This sent my little stain hater into hysterics. He'd fuss and fume

BARN DOORS

for me to "wipe it off," to which I would declare, "Honey, there is no wiping her off."

He grew up to be a stain-hating teenager too. Every hair had to be in place, every microscopic fiber of lint rolled off his wrinkle-free clothes. Until he moved back to the States when he was fifteen to finish high school. I warned him that the Midwest was muddy, and he was going to the country. He didn't even own a pair of mud boots. He lived with Grandma and Grandpa, and while he may have started out as a stain-hating teenager, his grandpa is quite the opposite, and my son got over his OCD of stains quick, fast, and in a hurry.

My three Little Loves aren't so little anymore. That's okay; there's not an age limit when it comes to love stains. If they'd hold still long enough, I'd slosh them real good with some of my own love stains. They don't dawdle much anymore, and they run faster than me. But I put puddles of love in their path that trip them as they run. There's more than one way to make a love stain stick.

Third Verse

What do the hymns "It Is Well with My Soul," "The Old Rugged Cross," and "Lead Me to Calvary" have in common? Their third verses carry enormous power—and my church skips them and many others during song service. After a year of singing with this church and omitting these third verses, my heart suddenly ached to know what I was missing.

I borrowed a hymnal and scoured through all my favorites, silently hitting the high notes, savoring the words that are eloquently strung together like the graceful, harmonious strum of a guitar.

My sin not in part, but the whole is nailed to the cross and I bear it no more. Praise the Lord, praise the Lord, O my soul.

In the old rugged cross, stained with blood so divine, such a wonderful beauty I see; for t'was on that old cross Jesus suffered and died, to pardon and sanctify me.

Let me like Mary, thro' the gloom, come with a gift to thee; show to me now the empty tomb, lead me to Calvary.

Barn Doors

Imagine a song service with nothing but missing third verses! We could call it the Third Verse Service and invite the congregation to look with fresh eyes at the wonder waiting to be discovered between those lines of ink. Lines of ink that are only words until we let them soothe an aching soul, lift a sagging heart, or anchor a wavering faith.

I never expected my heart to embrace the hymn-singing style song service found in the church where God put me. Praise music used to be such a driving force in how I worshiped while living overseas. There I attended a church with a fast-beat contemporary style of worship where the music lifted my hands for me, tears trickled down my face of their own accord, and song books were never needed.

This is still a powerful way for me to voice my praises to God, but having room in my heart for both styles is what surprises me. I always thought I was an all-or-nothing kind of gal, but God continues to stretch me and show me that He loves both, so why can't I? The heart of worship reaches His ears even before the words do. Many times the words choke me up, rendering my voice useless. I count on my heart to worship for me in those times.

I also pray that I never forget the blessings I've received from being plunked down in a hymn-singing church. I pray the sweet voices from the older generation always make me smile, and I always ponder a little more closely the things that remain ageless:

- There is still power in the blood of Jesus.
- Grannies still leave lipstick on baby cheeks.
- The cup and bread are still passed in remembrance of Jesus's sacrifice.

- My sin is still nailed to the Cross, not in part but the whole.
- The Word of God is still preached from the pulpit.
- Easter hats are still worn by little girls on Easter morning.
- Jesus still loves me, this I know.
- Voices still quaver when a song touches deep.
- Church ladies still cook the best potluck dinners.
- The Lord is still my Shepherd, and in pastures green He leadeth me.
- Pews still hold hurting souls—altars too.
- Little hands still fold when Sunday school teachers pray.

Amazing grace still saves wretches like me.

Stickers in the Sky

White lies are little, harmless, and "everyone tells them." They have a way of just slipping out, and there is very little decision-making that takes place beforehand. Reasons for telling them range from "Santa is watching you," all the way down to "You look great in that dress!" They articulate of their own accord when patting a crying friend's shoulder and saying, "There, there, it's not that bad." Husbands dote on their wives' cooking while choking down every bite of their least favorite dish.

No big deal. Telling little white lies doesn't keep us up at night. It doesn't make us bad people.

They are so easy to tell–they slip out unchecked and often unnoticed. But I have a story to prove just how damaging little white lies are to your integrity.

Many years ago, a friend's teenage son takes a trip from France to England. Everyone boards the plane; he finds his seat. There's always some chaos when settling in, buckling up, storing bags overhead—elbows and tight quarters, you get the idea. Even for short flights, the chaos does not diminish by much compared to longer ones.

This teen goes through the unavoidable and chaotic ritual with his fellow flying mates aboard the plane (I used *mates* because he's British. Ha!). He then notices a sticker on the back of the seat in front of him. It's one of those that are passed out in a fun pack for little ones to entertain them during the flight. I'm sure the edges were rubbed off where the crew probably attempted to remove it but gave up when it left behind that nasty residue that stickers are notorious for.

While waiting for flight hostesses to lock up so the pilot could back away from the terminal, my friend's son hears an announcement that the plane is having mechanical difficulties and everyone would have to disembark and take their belongings with them.

Imagine the chaotic ritual in reverse.

After a lengthy period of time, everyone is allowed to board a new plane that does not have any mechanical issues. The hostesses who greet the frazzled passengers assure them this is a different plane and all checked luggage has been transferred. There's nothing to worry about. The pilot, I'm sure, insisted on a new plane because the safety of those in his care was of the utmost importance.

I can hear the sighs of relief, the assurance folks felt as they began the chaotic ritual again: settling in, buckling up, storing bags overhead—elbows and tight quarters, you get the idea. My friend's son takes his seat and comes face to face with a sticker on the back of the seat in front of him.

Any chance this is a freak coincidence? Did every plane of this particular airline have a kiddie sticker on the back of 26B's seat? Of course not. Flight personnel told a little white lie. No big deal. The intent was to ease any fear the passengers may have felt.

But white lies with good intentions are still lies. When found out, they feel like betrayal.

Barn Doors

This is a different plane with no mechanical issues? Really? You mean Santa is not real? And this dress actually makes my butt look a mile wide? You seriously can't stand chicken pot pie? I've made it *every week* for thirteen years because *you said* you loved it!

———•———

Good intentions don't come to the surface when a white lie is finally uncovered. No, betrayal comes to the surface, and your integrity disintegrates before your eyes. With trust in the little things now broken, trust in the big things is near impossible. Like those notoriously sticky stickers, white lies can leave residue in a relationship that we pick at during every flight we take.

I won't leave behind a remnant of theology for this chapter, just encouragement to keep trusting, but also to be someone others can trust in the big things as well as the little things. I know, you're all shocked to discover Santa isn't real. He's not, but the Fixer of broken things *is* real. Trust me.

"Whoever can be trusted with very little can also be trusted with much, and whoever is dishonest with very little will also be dishonest with much" (Luke 16:10).

Bald Tooth Fairy

Arms crossed, I stand with my back against a closed door, pouting. Things aren't going my way. My life has fallen apart, and control is no longer mine. Was it ever mine? I've closed Him out. After all, He deserves it; it's His fault I'm hurting. But...I still need Him in some areas of my life, so I only shut the door on painful places in my heart. Places I don't trust Him to carry me through. The suffering is too great. A piece of paper brushes against my bare foot and I reach down. Little hearts color one side; poems, promises, and words of love cover the other side. Before I finish reading, another sheet of paper touches my foot. God—Creator of the universe—is slipping me love notes under the door. ~ excerpt from the "Love Notes" chapter in *Broken Umbrellas* (WhiteFire Publishing, 2015)

God gave me this beautiful image of slipping me love notes several years ago while I processed the news that my best friend had cancer. If you read *Broken Umbrellas*, then you already know I shaved my head for my friend, and that she is now cancer free. Just so you don't have to wonder through this entire story, yes, I'm the bald tooth fairy.

God is a multi-tasker. I say this because it's been true in my life.

Barn Doors

His blessings have a tumbling effect and knock those in the path off their feet—in a good way. Shaving my head was one such time where God multi-tasked His blessing.

Before shaving my head, I spent several weeks praying about it. It would have been meaningless if God didn't get the glory and it didn't touch my friend. I included my daughter—who was nine at the time—in the pondering process, being open with her and asking for her thoughts. She didn't have any serious issues one way or the other. She was very supportive, telling me to do what I needed to do for my friend. We talked about our value as women and where that comes from. Certainly not from our hair.

She watched my hair fall to the floor, and I studied her face for signs of trauma. She was unfazed, but she did agree that my eyebrows grew instantly with no hair above them to make things balanced.

As luck would have it, she lost a tooth right after I shaved my head. Her first reaction was, "Oh, great! My tooth fairy is bald!" and then she fell into a fit of giggles. It became a joke between us. Actually, she became quite versed in all things bald-joke related.

Sometime after the bald tooth fairy visited my daughter, she got aggravated at her own hair for falling into her eyes when she sat Indian-style with a book in her lap. She picked it straight up and whacked it off. Right in front where her cowlick was most prominent. It looked hideous. When I saw it, I gasped. Any normal, non-bald mother would have. She raised an eyebrow, tilted her head, and looked from my face to the top of my head as if to say, "Really? You're shocked?" Yeah, I know. The bald mother gasped in shock when her daughter whacked off a chunk of her own hair.

We laughed the kind of laughing where your sides hurt and just one look from the other sends you both into hysterics again. In my defense, it was a normal reaction. In her defense, I had just preached about how hair is not what defines us as women.

Hair defines you as a woman in the minds of others, however. Like our hairdresser who did not gasp several weeks later when he saw my daughter's self-inflicted haircut, but he did fret—verbally—about not being equipped to fix such a disaster. I told him we were there just for a trim, that what was done was done. Let it be. He did not let it be. He fussed over her cowlick, talking under his breath, and I regretted not trimming it myself. I felt like he had undone everything I had spent so much time pouring into my daughter about her worth and where that comes from.

We had a refresher course after we left the beauty shop.

Shaving my head was the best thing I ever did. It blessed my friend who struggled deeply because the choice of whether or not to lose her hair had been taken away from her. Shaving my head blessed my relationship with my daughter and continues to do so as we remember those bald days and hair-whacking days. Now that she's a teenager, it's all about messy-bun days, or braided-pigtail days.

I take my time braiding her hair. It's long. It's thick. I'd be lying if I said her hair wasn't important to her. It usually is at this age. But I pray when she grows up, she has at least one special friend whom she wouldn't hesitate to shave her head for. I pray she knows that kind of deep connection that threads friendship hearts together so tightly, that what hurts one hurts the other. Whether that friend faces cancer, a difficult marriage, or loss of some sort, I pray my daughter is the kind of friend who doesn't let her friend carry the burdens alone.

And I pray *her* daughter whacks her own hair off and it makes *my* daughter gasp.

Candy As a Love Language

It's hard to believe, but I promise it's true. Candy is a love language. I was once a doubter. Not anymore. There's too much proof! Let me prove it to you.

First, we have to figure out what the term "love language" even means. A love language is what communicates love to you. I want to be clear—yes, there's a guy and he wrote a book about some love languages.[1] It's very popular and has helped tons of couples speak the right love language to communicate love to their spouses. I have that book. I love that book. And I'm not minimizing that book in any way by suggesting candy is a love language. His book opened my eyes, ears, and heart to the concept of love languages. Now I more easily recognize love when it is communicated—as well as pay attention to *how* it is communicated.

My daughter loves candy. Like, a crazy kind of love—addicting and sweet. She's loved it from toddlerhood. And she still loves it as a teenager. It's such a crazy love that a few years ago I bought her a wooden plaque that says: IT'S ALL ABOUT THE CANDY. If you want to communicate love to her, buy her a bag of candy. Candy is her love language.

Being her mama through the sugar highs of having a love language like candy, I've picked up on some subtleties that are actually quite powerful. Even powerful enough to prompt me to write about it for *Barn Doors*. Powerful enough that I want to prove to you that candy is a love language.

Candy is not my daughter's only love language. It's pretty dominant, though, and I first noticed it when she was three. She drew a picture of Jesus, putting lots of detail and concentration into the drawing. When she was finished, she announced in English, "Jesus is candy!" Very impressive because she is bilingual and, at the age of three, was not forming complete sentences in either language but rather using a mix of both languages until she was five-and-a-half.

This is a good place to tell you that I'm writing a children's series called The Keeper Series. Each of the three books is dedicated to my three children. My daughter's book is being illustrated as I write this very paragraph. In the story dedicated to her, I have incorporated that link between Jesus and candy.

Is there a link between our little love languages and the Creator of love? Psalm 139 describes how God knit us together. Everything about us can be linked to our Creator—from our eyelashes to our love languages.

Interesting thing about love languages—not only do you need your love language spoken to you to feel love, but you speak that language to others as a way to communicate your love to them. Even if it's not their love language. That guy who wrote the book on love languages covers this interesting phenomenon. We have to be intentional to speak another person's love language if we want to communicate love to them.

But that's too deep for toddlers. They speak what they speak. Candy was already a powerful love language for my daughter at age three, and Jesus was candy to her. That's all she needed to understand.

Just like adults speak the love language they need spoken to them, my daughter did the same. If I'd had prior insight into just how powerful this thing would be, I would have taken a lot more notes back then, journaled extensively. But alas, I only have one solid example that fits perfectly right here, which I remember in full detail. Trust me, it alone is proof enough.

When she was four, I hit a wall of depression that bound me to bed in absolute misery. It did not last long, but the few days it did were a nightmare. If I was awake, I was crying. If I was asleep, I was unconscious to the world around me. I woke up somewhere in the middle of day three to find my daughter placing a ring of gummy bears in my hair. She melted my heart as she spoke the most beautiful mix of French and English over me: "*Les bonbons* (candy) make you feel better."

Did I throw gummy bears across the room and insist she speak my love language and go fetch me a cup of coffee? You better believe I listened to her love language, and those gummy bears did indeed get me up out of that bed with a smile on my face.

Yes, be intentional—when you're all grown-up—and make efforts to speak the specific love language of those in your life so they feel your love for them. But also speak the love language you need *from* them. This shows them who you are, what you need, and also how to speak it.

I love cards! I feel so much love when someone takes the time to give me a card. If I constantly gave cards to someone who would feel more love receiving candy, and they constantly gave me candy when I feel more love receiving cards, there's not much love being felt. Love is being spoken, but is it being felt to the full capacity?

Speaking of cards. I have a friend who used to send me care packages when I lived in France. Those boxes were the biggest blessings ever. One in particular was close to my birthday. There was a sealed card inside. I opened it and found a card that wasn't even signed. It was hilarious! I asked her about it and she didn't realize she'd forgotten to sign it before sealing it. I love that card so much. It makes me laugh every time I think about it. It truly is the thought that communicates love to me, not the actual signed card.

I'm sure for my daughter, however, it isn't just the *thought* of candy that communicates love to her. She needs others to know how much she loves candy and for them to offer it to her. She also needs to feel the squishiness of gummies, taste the sugar that coats her tongue, and see those bright colors and fun shapes. The pleasure of taking the tongs in the candy store, lifting the candy lid, and dropping the right number of candies into her sack make up the details of that sweet language. She needs candy offered to her on a rough day, sticking out of her stocking, and shared with friends on birthdays.

Parenting a candy-loving child has been tricky. That's why weekly visits to the candy store caused me to quickly come up with a plan for just how many were allowed. The right number of candies she could have corresponded with her age. When she was 3, she could choose three. When she was 6, she could choose six.

Are you convinced? Did I present enough proof for you to believe candy is a love language? What little details in your life make you feel loved? Do the people around you know them? Do you know

Barn Doors

the little details that make them feel loved? Get that guy's book. It's powerful. While you're waiting for it to arrive in the mail, go ahead and ponder the seemingly insignificant love languages that speak love to you and people around you. Trust me, they are not insignificant. They have the power to connect you with the Creator of love.

I want Jesus to always be candy to my daughter. Just like the *thought* of candy alone does not fully speak love, Jesus can't just be thought about—He needs to be felt, tasted, seen. What a beautiful link candy makes to Jesus. I'm willing to bet your little love languages connect you to Jesus too.

Grace and Law Collide

For Michael

Weight of the law
Pierce the heart
Where sin reigns
And rules the dark

Darkness shrinks
If sin comes to light
If washed in the blood
If wrong is made right

Right has a name
His arms open wide
He waits at the Cross
Where grace and law collide

Barn Doors

Letter of the law
Write on the heart
With hopeless ink
And convicting marks

Marks that draw
A line in the sand
For a choice to be made
Where a sinner now stands

Stand over there
Or step to My side
Where the ink of sin fades
When grace and law collide

———•———

Waters of grace
Rush over the heart
With waves of mercy
On a born-again start

A start that arrives
On the winds of change
When a heart chooses Christ
And carries His flame

The flame of salvation
Though the world tries to hide

Is offered to all
Because grace and law collide

———•———

Drops of pure grace
Drench broken hearts
That journey to healing
From enemy darts

Darts meant to cripple
To keep feet astray
From the peace that comes
With God's saving grace

Grace covers law
Spirit will abide
In the depths of a believer
Where grace and law collide

———•———

Chords of sweet grace
Touch faithful hearts
When law dictates:
"Don't fall apart"

Do fall apart
Let pieces scatter
None will be lost

Barn Doors

For God will gather

And gather He does
For the sake of His bride
Love conquers all
When grace and law collide

And the Word became flesh, and dwelt among us, and we saw His glory, glory as of the only begotten from the Father, full of grace and truth.... For of His fullness we have all received, and grace upon grace. For the Law was given through Moses; grace and truth were realized through Jesus Christ (John 1:14, 16-17 NASB, emphasis added).

Birthday Buddy

Everybody has one; mine just so happens to love God as much as I do. I found her quite by accident. A glorious, God-orchestrated accident.

She'd side-swiped a pole at the grocery store before coming to Awana—where we met—to pick up her kids. I didn't even know her name; I just grabbed that frazzled bundle of upset and hugged her tight and prayed for her in the church parking lot. And that's how it started.

Awana made our paths cross once a week that 2010 school year—me working with Cubbies, her dropping off and picking up her four children. Through the course of drop off/pick up salutations, we discovered that we shared a June birthday.

My forty-first birthday was celebrated at an Indian restaurant with her across from me. With a fork full of food mere inches from my mouth, I asked her how old she was. Forty-one. I paused, fork midair, and thought about that. If I was forty-one, and she was forty-one, we didn't just share a birth date, we were real live birthday buddies!

Barn Doors

We got so tickled when we discovered that we were also born the same year. The most delightful part of all is that she was born in the Philippines, I was born in Iowa, and we met in France. After studying our birth certificates and figuring time zone differences, we calculated that she was born two hours before me.

My birthday buddy loves to cook; I love to eat her cooking. She loves to paint; I love to hang her paintings on my wall. She pours shredded cheese into a bowl with a spoon for serving; I toss the bag on the table. She has no sense of direction; I hop out of the car and parallel park her car for her. She starts a joke and can't finish it; I laugh because *she* is so funny. She loves all things blue; I love all things green. She stops and smells the roses; I stop and smell the roses—but she doesn't move on until she's taken twenty-seven pictures of those roses.

Besides sharing a birthday, we are as opposite as her darker skin is to my lighter skin. Until we start talking about Jesus—then you can't tell us apart. We both have compassion as deep as an ocean. We both live the motto "Love Jesus, Love People." The same things bring us to tears, bring us to our knees in prayer. We read the Bible together, hold hands and intercede for someone in need together, visit the homeless together, sing in the car together. Our conversations are God-centered and God-pleasing, and I always leave her presence uplifted and complete.

My birthday buddy side-swiped that pole at just the right time. God orchestrated her arrival to coincide with a season of my life where she would be most valued and most loved. A season of radical healing from deep-rooted brokenness. I speak about that season in my nonfiction book *Broken Umbrellas*. I am who I am today because of that season. As God worked on changing me from the inside out, He placed gifts in my life. Gifts like a hand-picked, hand-delivered birthday buddy to walk this journey with me. As He emptied me of harmful beliefs, emotions, and mindsets, He filled me with everlasting treasures like the ability to recognize a gift from His own heart as well as the ability to care for that gift. What a comfort it is to know we will always be birthday buddies, always be sisters in Christ, and always give God the glory.

Now, wait until you hear about our forty-sixth birthday!

Friendship Tree

Birthdays and friends go together better than cake and ice cream. There's something special about welcoming another year with a friend by your side. Before my forties, those friends added the flare and spice and fun to the celebration. Now into my forties, they are necessary to hold my hand, wipe my aging tears, and help me blow out the candles because I can no longer get them all in one breath.

A few years ago, a friend forgot to acknowledge my birthday. When she realized it, she apologized to the moon and back. I assured her forgetting my birthday was by far the best gift anyone had ever given me. It's now a yearly joke between us.

On the other side of the birthday coin, my birthday buddy never forgets my birthday. She adds the flare and spice, despite my desire to forget sometimes that I'm yet another year older. Like our recent celebration at La Pataterie—a glorious potato restaurant in France. First, this particular birthday buddy (okay, she's my only birthday buddy), asked the waitress to take our photo while motioning for me to scoot around to her side—much to the amusement of everyone in the place. I then returned to my seat across from her with thoughts like, *Only a birthday buddy could get away with that.*

Our potato dishes arrived with all the flare and cheese to make this a mouth-watering celebration indeed. And then, that birthday buddy of mine ordered dessert. Did she just let our birthdays slide by discreetly? Of course not! She told the waitress it was our birthday, and the waitress asked if she'd like the staff to sing for us. And how would any flare-loving, larger-than-life, never-boring birthday buddy answer? *Why, yes please! That would be amazing.* And while utterly dramatic and the opposite of discreet, it was truly amazing. A candle stuck into a marshmallow appeared before her, and before me a sparkler mocked my age with its pizzazz-y fun sizzle. I couldn't help myself; I laughed. And it was fun. Half a dozen waiters and waitresses sang, my birthday buddy and I blew out that single candle together, and everyone clapped. Then I scooped up crème brûlée and decided right then and there that every birthday for the rest of my life should be celebrated with crème brûlée, candles, and friends who add the burning flames.

This past summer, my daughter celebrated her twelfth birthday in France with both her French and American families. And while that was wonderful, her little heart ached to blow out the candles with her friends surrounding her. I promised her a party when we returned stateside, and while I write this I am planning that party. Nine friends are invited—nine larger-than-life friends. My daughter has given me complete freedom in ordering her cake, allowing me to surprise her with its decorations.

The last few months, I've been thinking back over the years and

Barn Doors

revisiting my own friendships. And what a journey my mind and heart have been on! Sweet memories, tons of laughs, a few regrets, even bits of sadness have rushed forth like a geyser. They crossed my mind in perfect perspective, with the older regretful ones more faded, and the bold, "friends forever" ones front and center. Drawing on these friendships—from the short-lived ones to the lasting ones—I have the perfect surprise for my daughter.

A friendship tree cake.

Imagine, if you will, a tree with hearts dangling like fruit. Each heart carries the name of a friend. And the text reads: CELEBRATING BIRTHDAYS WITH FRIENDS IS BETTER THAN EATING CAKE. Because it's true. That's all she wanted for her birthday, for her friends to welcome her twelfth year with her. Acknowledge her and celebrate with flare, giggles, and fun.

The possibility is high that all nine of these friends will not help usher in her forty-sixth birthday. Maybe not even her thirteenth. But this year, they will. And she is elated. I keep my own friendship memories for myself, allowing her to experience and collect the sweet memories, laughs, regrets, and even sadness that decades of friendships will bring. It all belongs on her friendship tree. The edible one she'll devour in a few days, and the metaphoric one she'll draw on and revisit when she's my age. New names will appear over the years, some blurry and distant, others bold and present. But all of them will dangle from her tree, with some fruit blossoms that grow while others wither and fall. With some roots that die while others reach astounding depths.

All God's Creatures

She was the love of my teenage son's life. Her name was Mosquito—and she was a rat. Love is love no matter who is on the receiving end, and trust me, a lot of love was invested into that six-dollar rodent. So when she got sick, I didn't hesitate to take her to the vet. After all, a broken heart was on the line.

When my oldest son was seventeen, he had growing pains like every kid his age. He'd needed me less and less through his adolescent years, and showing him that I loved him had become a challenge. That's why I prayed God would give me the opportunity to touch my son in a special way. Little did I know at the time that the answer would present itself in the form of a rat.

I remember the day Mosquito moved in. One autumn morning, in a crowded store—where I couldn't have a mama hissy fit—my son came to me with a pleading look and asked me to buy him a rat. I said no, but he begged until I finally said I would think about it. He left to go "lick the aquarium glass." Window shopping in French translates "lick the glass." I know, it's not funny if I have to explain it.

Anyway, back to my internal mama hissy fit. I thought long and hard. I tried to focus on the health issues and the responsibility that went along with having a rat living in the house. But the only thing that entered my heart and mind was that my son needed something to love. It's hard for teenagers to show their feelings, open up, and talk to their parents—express themselves. If a rat could wiggle into his heart and produce positive feelings, it had to be therapeutic for a hormone-raged boy/man.

We bought the rat, and it was a race to see if we'd make it home before she chewed her way out of the cardboard box. She won. And my furry rodent nightmares began.

One day, I entered my son's room to collect dirty socks. As I bent over, I noticed that Mosquito's cage was open and she wasn't inside. I froze with one foot in the air. (I added that for dramatic flair.) Panic gripped me. My heart raced as my eyes darted around the room. I took a deep breath. (More dramatic flair.) I had to stay calm. Think rationally. I quickly put the cat in the bathroom and shut the door. (Yes, we had a cat. He moved in before the rat.) The last thing I wanted was for Mosquito to be lunch. I wasn't worried about her being lunch, per se, just worried that I'd have to clean up the leftovers.

I then searched my son's bedroom from top to bottom. I looked in boxes. Under pillows. Inside shoes. I found lots of things I didn't want to find—but no rat. I stood by her cage and tried to visualize the path she would have taken. Hanging nearby was a variety of clothing and coats. Was it possible? I tiptoed to the rack and stopped within arm's length. I took a deep breath. Slowly, I reached out and opened my son's winter coat. There she was, curled up in a ball inside the armpit.

Love is love, no matter who is on the receiving end. She loved my son and missed him while he was at school. His scent comforted her. Love drove me to scoop her up (Eek!) and gently place her back where she belonged. Not love for her, but for my son. He loved her, I love him. It was that simple.

From that moment, I became more lenient when Mosquito ventured out of her cage, usually on his shoulder, although I put my foot down when she joined us for meals.

Over time, tiny sores developed around Mosquito's face. Together, my son and I nursed her and applied ointment. They didn't heal and she stopped eating. He was worried and broken-hearted. "She's going to die, Mom."

"Not if we can help it," I said. "She just needs to see the vet."

"The vet?" He stared at me as if I were from outer space.

"Sure. That's what vets are for."

"She's just a rat," he said with a hint of hope in his voice.

"No, son. She's not just a rat."

By the look in his eyes, I knew I had touched that place inside of him that hadn't been touched in a long time. If I had thought before I'd spoken, I would've told him a new rat was cheaper than a vet bill. But then the opportunity to show I cared would have passed by.

We arrived at the vet's office. A man with a cat arrived at the same time. Though we were anxious, we held the door for him, and he walked up to the desk.

"Have a seat with your cat," the vet said as she motioned us around him. "The rat has an appointment."

The vet took her time examining Mosquito, even weighed her. She prescribed antibiotics for abscessed teeth. "She needs to see a dentist."

My mouth fell open. "A *rat* dentist?"

My mouth fell even further when I heard the fee. Astronomical. We could buy a rat farm for the price of extracting two rodent teeth.

Barn Doors

We paid the vet bill then left with antibiotics and a referral.

We couldn't afford to extract Mosquito's teeth, so we began to pray. After several days, Mosquito began to heal. She started to eat again. We continued the antibiotics and the prayer.

Mosquito lived a long life nibbling French cheese. She smoothed the rough edges of my son's adolescence. Even in a rage, he melted when she was near. He patiently got her out of tight corners when she explored his room. He fed her and smothered her with love and affection.

He cared for her in the same way that I care for him—in the same way that God cares for him. From teenagers to rodents, we're all God's creatures. He holds each of us in His hand, even when the world might call us unworthy of such care.

Snarky Tension

Several years ago, I battled—and won—an ungodly spirit toward smokers. It still rears its ugly head every once in a while, but I just close my eyes and repeat, "Hate the habit, love the person. Hate the habit, love the person."

My daughter is asthmatic. When she was six, her father and I divorced. He's a smoker. I spent the next four years fighting her asthma crises that were brought on by exposure to second-hand smoke. Her pulmonologist reprimanded her father by letter. The pediatrician scolded him to his face—more than once. I nagged. My daughter cried and complained to him. And yet he continued to put her in harm's way. After spending a weekend in a smoke-infested environment and coming home with a full-on attack, she would sometimes be too sick to attend school the next day.

We were living in Europe at the time, and the government didn't find it a child endangerment issue—just snarky tension between divorced parents. Needless to say, this made me very bitter and furious that there was nothing I could do but send her out the door knowing that when she came back, she would be in a terrible state.

We also didn't have a vehicle and lived a mile up the side

Barn Doors

of a mountain with switchbacks and ninety-five steep stairs to climb before arriving—by foot—at our door. I will say that public transportation in Europe is phenomenal and easy to use. Before moving back to the States, my daughter and I got around in Europe for four years via trams, buses, and our own two feet. Which was a great way to stay in shape...unless you had asthma. Getting my daughter to the doctor required getting her down the mountain to the bus stop at the bottom and also back up the mountain afterward. I often pushed my elementary-aged child in a stroller. Bitterness grew to new levels the more I had to push her up the mountain.

While her father was the biggest source of her asthma attacks, he wasn't the only source. Sitting at bus stops, we were inundated with cigarette smoke. We opted to stand outside the bus stop in the freezing cold and/or rain because smokers were so insensitive to those around them. My daughter even suffered a major crisis one winter day, and I asked a smoker to be considerate. He moved three steps to his left and continued smoking. I quickly took her out of the shelter and into the freezing rain where she vomited because her air was cut off and she struggled to cough and breathe. I pumped medication into her, trying to keep her under an umbrella to no avail.

And the hill of bitterness grew into a mountain. I snarled my lip and glared at every smoker I passed—even if my daughter wasn't with me. I had no patience for smokers, said snide comments under my breath when they littered their cigarette butts in the park where children played. I would cough exaggeratedly, waving my hand in front of my face. I confronted a few. Most ignored me or said nasty things in return. Only a handful in four years cared enough to put out their cigarette or move away from the cross breeze.

Only a thin line separates intolerance and hate. And I started hating smokers. I caught myself every time and flooded my mind and heart with truth—that it was the habit I hated, not the person.

Aside from all this, I was a Christian with a heart for evangelism. How on earth was I ever going to witness to a non-Christian smoker with my heart hardened toward them because of their addiction? How was I representing Christ with a snarled lip and snide comments? Have you ever tried to pass someone a friendly smile when your forehead is wrinkled with disdain and your eyes are glaring? It does not work, trust me.

Hate the habit, love the person. I spent months repeating this to myself at every bus and tram stop, outside shops, on every street corner, or while sitting at an outside table eating lunch.

God, in His humorous way, didn't feel my little chant was heartfelt enough. One day I had to pick up a package from the post office. My daughter went with me and took her allowance because she knew there was a tobacco shop right beside the post office. Tobacco shops in Europe are where you find the really cool magazines, and the kids' magazines come in plastic wrap with a toy inside. I signed for the package, got it into my grocery utility cart—what folks do when they don't have a car—and we headed over to the tobacco shop. This particular one was long and narrow, barely enough room to scoot sideways down its two isles. There was no way to get the cart in the store, so I left it on the sidewalk outside the door and stood just inside the shop to keep an eye on my daughter and the cart at the same time.

The only way I could avoid blocking customers was to open the door for them. Of course, I greeted them with a "good day," and they returned the greeting. After opening the tobacco shop door a dozen times to allow a dozen smokers to enter and buy their cigarettes, the irony of it all hit me and I doubled over laughing.

Barn Doors

Humbling me to the point of serving these once-detested people was exactly what God needed to do to get my attention. Ugliness in my heart toward smokers vanished. I found myself praying a few more smokers would patronize the shop just so I could open the door for them.

Then I really put my heart into it and greeted them with not only a "good day" but also a heartfelt smile.

Sock Ministry

I love to fold socks, and it's a ministry. What makes it a ministry is that I fold socks for friends. I've been known to wash bags of dirty ones too. Just for the fun of mating them—and to show my friends how much I love them.

Admit it: folding socks is like washing silverware by hand. Everyone hates it! If you don't hate folding socks, call me. We'll go into ministry together. You can fold all the white ones! I like matching up the fun colorful ones.

The idea of ministry can be so limited. Let's explore outside the box and see where it takes us. Actually, if I were one of *those* writers, I'd make a laundry joke right now and say something like, "Let's explore outside the dryer and see where the lint trail takes us." But I'm not one of those writers, so we'll use a box.

Ministry—let's ignore society's restricted definition of it being for folks with theological degrees—simply means "a provided service that is charitable or spiritual in nature." Voilà! Folding socks for people is a service. Folding socks for people is charitable. And folding socks for people is spiritual.

Barn Doors

Yes, spiritual. I make it spiritual. I pray for the feet that go into those socks. The little feet of a friend's children, the big feet of her spouse.

A minister of all things sock-related cannot march into a friend's home and demand to see her basket of unmated socks. That is something usually hidden in a closet or spare bedroom—even hidden from the best of friends. No one talks about the basket of unmated socks. A minister of sock folding must gain the trust of that friend. I have done this a couple of different ways.

One is to address the issue indirectly, exaggeratedly talking about your basket of unmated socks sitting at home waiting for you. This assures the friend that she is not the only one who has an abundance of unmated socks. After the sock is out of the closet, so to speak, finish your visit but mention the unmated socks the next time you're there. Subtly of course! The best approach is to tell the friend—after she's admitted the visit before to having her own basket of unmated socks—that you want to do something nice for her. It would bless you tremendously to bless her. And she wouldn't want to keep God's blessings from you, now would she? She'll insist there is nothing you can do to bless her other than sitting with a cup of tea and chatting with her. *Having you for a friend is all the blessing I need.* Counter this with a list of possible ways you could bless her. Mow the grass, get her groceries, fold her socks, or wash her windows. Notice how everything but the socks is very labor intensive. Trust me, she'll pick folding socks every time. Besides, that's something you can do while drinking tea.

Another way that has proven effective for me is to go into the home of a friend recuperating after surgery and just fold her socks! This worked for one friend, and I spent the entire time assuring her I really loved doing it! I explained how it was a ministry for me to mate and fold my friends' socks. Giggle of all giggles, the next time I visited, she'd saved her unmated socks and brought them out one evening after supper and said, "If you wanted to fold my socks while we watched a movie, that'd be okay." Good grief, I love her.

That same friend, while I visited one day, busied herself in the kitchen then came up behind me on the loveseat and said, "Lean forward." She slid a warm water bottle down my back and leaned me against it. When I left that visit, she gave me the water bottle. I told her she had a water bottle ministry. Then again, everything she does is a ministry because she loves on people as naturally as she breathes.

I have another precious friend who makes soup for people, when they're sick or just because. Every spoonful of soup goes down like a spoonful of her love. She has a soup ministry. A lady in my church has a birthday card ministry. Love poured out in a personal way that touches people around you—that's another way to define ministry.

Are you a minister of something seemingly insignificant? Approach that ministry in a new light and see it for what it truly is—a real, larger-than-life ministry.

From Paris to Potholes

The Louvre stood before us, majestic and...huge! We stepped across ancient cobblestones, eager to explore the treasures waiting for us inside. Humanity of every shape and size, color and nationality rubbed elbows with us. We fought the masses to capture a photo of the *Mona Lisa*. Our feet climbed winding stone steps and walked along echoing corridors. Souvenirs hung in bags from our arms while history hung in frames around us.

My daughter and I wasted not one second of our day in Paris before flying back home to the Midwest. Three raindrops fell on us as we patronized shop after crowded shop along Rue du Rivoli, dined at a brasserie, and ate ice cream in front of the Eiffel Tower. A waiter served us a glass of *sirop* at a busy café while we filled out last-minute postcards, and a beggar played a song for us on the RER train between our hotel and the center of Paris. We squeezed into subways with fashionable, wrinkle-free French mothers, children eating apricots, and businessmen on their way home from work.

Every second of Parisian culture soaked into us as fast as we could sponge it up. For we knew the next morning promised a long flight before we reentered Midwestern life.

Never are the diverse parallels between these two worlds more evident than when one goes from strolling the streets of Paris to driving over the potholes of my town. Switching gears becomes a challenge, and it takes me time to stop saying *bonjour* and start saying hello again. I need a moment or two of self-pity when going from fresh baguettes to factory-made sliced bread. No longer do I blend in with the crowd as "Madame," now I'm everyone's "sweetheart" and "honey." Not that I mind being called sweetheart and honey by complete strangers. I love it very much! It's the switch that causes me to hesitate and ponder.

Hesitate and ponder how it's possible to be so completely immersed in one culture that to go back into another is a drastic shock. After only a month!

Switching gears going the other way is just as pronounced. Washing machines that take an hour, no air conditioning, using public transportation, no customer service. But it doesn't take as long for me to adjust. Nor do I mind the sacrifices. And I wonder why.

I placed my feet on American soil only four years ago after living in France for fourteen. Balance between loving both cultures so immensely will surely come, but not without some bumps and bruises to my emotions. I must breathe in grace when I struggle to adjust. Stop fretting that I'm somehow a different person there than I am here. I didn't leave Jesus on the streets of Paris, nor did I return to find Him skipping over potholes. He went with me, stayed with me, and returned with me because living in Christ isn't a switch from one culture to another. It's constant and steady. Actually, it's the only constant and steady element when one's heart resides in two places at once.

Barn Doors

Like living as a Christ-follower in this world without being of this world. When we are here, yet our eyes are focused on there. Rubbing elbows with all forms of humanity while our hearts cry for heaven.

My thoughts often turn to the diversity of life on Earth and the promise of eternal life in heaven. How comfortable I sometimes get here—with God's glory and beauty around me—and the anticipation of life with God free of this world's hurts and wounds. Just when I get comfortable, strolling along the cobblestones of my life, I hear a story of humanity hurting humanity, and I beg Jesus to come rescue His Church. I go back and forth, and the switching in my heart is always difficult. To love God's creation and the life He has given me on earth, yet to ache so much for Him to come and end all suffering.

The hotel shuttle took my daughter and me to Charles de Gaulle that last morning in France. We discussed our month in France, the things we would miss, the things we looked forward to in America. We shared our favorite highlights of the previous day in Paris and how it was hard to leave this country we both loved so much.

We had traveled with my daughter's French passport because her American passport had expired. We obtained the signed permission forms from her father during our month in France, and I had photocopies of her birth certificate and expired American passport. The airline could not print my daughter's boarding pass. It took an hour, with phone calls to the embassy, overriding systems, changing expiration dates, and shuffling us from one agent to another. During our frazzled hour, I felt peace that God was in control. I prayed for His immediate intervention, and thanked Him that somehow I had allowed enough time for this hiccup in our travels.

My daughter, on the other hand, did not feel that peace. She panicked, tears rolling down her face. And her words broke my earthly heart. "Mama, get me out of this country."

Amen, and amen again. "Come, Jesus, get us out of this hurting world."

Cake Crumbs and Sequins

Nothing humbles a heart more than cleaning a toilet. Just two days after the Facebook launch party for my nonfiction book *Broken Umbrellas*, I was cleaning the toilets at the Baptist church in a neighboring town. Someone asked me after the Facebook party if I ever came down off that party high. "Yup," I told them, "cleaning toilets took care of that!"

I've been this church's custodian since March 2015. Erected in 1888, this little country church is so precious to me, and so are the people who worship there. I vacuum their dust bunnies, wipe fingerprints from mirrors, straighten their hymnals, and yes, clean their toilets. I pray over the pews, for those who find safe haven in the house of God. As I wipe Kool-Aid from the kitchen counters, I imagine the children who come and quench their thirst. I straighten coloring pages and chairs in classrooms, pick up chalk and pennies, and praise God for these teachers shepherding their young flocks. I leave that place tired and with achy muscles but also with a peace that soothes my tired and achy heart.

The funny thing about peace is that you find it in the most peculiar places, sometimes doing the most mundane tasks. I've told myself "if only" so many times in my life. If only I made more money, then I would find peace. If only I weren't so busy, then I would find peace. If only I could clear my schedule, sit on that beach, make up with that person. If only I could quiet the chaos in my mind, heal my wounded heart, find a soothing balm for my battered soul. Then I would find peace. And I do find peace. Or rather, more times than not, peace finds me.

Earlier this summer, I found myself in a race against the clock to leave for a trip to France. The list of things to do grew, and I added more to the list than I marked off. Cleaning the Baptist church after VBS was one thing on that list. I've had the blessed honor of participating twice now in my own church's VBS, so I know the preparations that go into pulling one off. And I know in my heart of hearts that the same preparations would happen if only one child attended.

Twenty children came last week to the Baptist church's VBS. I know because I vacuumed up their cake crumbs and sequins. I cleaned their sticky glue prints and Kool-Aid stains. I found lost items and overflowing trash cans. I arrived frazzled because of everything still pending on my to-do list for France. I left at peace. And the only thing that happened between arriving and leaving was me cleaning.

Humility isn't a taker—it's a giver.

That's a new concept for me because I have always believed being humble—or humbled—required a sacrifice on my end. Something is taken from me. And sometimes it does, but leaving the church after VBS showed me that in humility, I receive far more than I ever give.

Peace. What a precious gift. It doesn't dangle just out of reach as we run around life's race track. It isn't something we work for, nor should it appear at the end of an "if only" sentence.

Peace is the natural consequence of a life lived in humility. God's

Barn Doors

gift to those who walk with Him, following Christ with integrity. Putting others first. Galatians 5:13 calls us to serve one another humbly in love. The result is a life of peace.

I did finally mark off the last thing on my to-do list before hopping on that plane. More nuggets of peace and humility were waiting for me on the other side of the pond. I stuffed them into my pockets and brought them home with me. Some appear in this book, sprinkled among the pages like a treasure hunt. My prayer is that peace finds you in the most unexpected ways. Grab them up and stuff them into *your* pockets.

I Find Peace

During that Facebook launch party for *Broken Umbrellas*, I asked the guests to help me finish a poem about peace and how to find it. Can I just say, y'all are poets! I love this project so much! Nothing rhymes, so don't go into this thinking it will jingle. Think deeper than that and hear the rhythms of hearts looking for peace.

NATURE

When the goose honks
And the grass sways
Then I will find peace

When the pond shimmers
Because the sun shines high
Then I will find peace

When the rain pours down
And its patter soothes me

Barn Doors

Then I will find peace

When the sun shines through clouds after the rain
And the rainbow arcs over the Alps
Then I will find peace

When the grass grows
And the flowers bloom
Then I will find peace

When the birds sing
And the beauty of the earth declares God's glory
Then I will find peace

When white clouds float across the blue of the sky
And the wind whispers in the trees
Then I will find peace

HOME, FRIENDS, FAMILY

When the neighbor comes calling
And the dog stops barking
Then I will find peace

When the house is quiet
And my soul is too
Then I will find peace

When my bed is made

Emma Broch Stuart

And my fruit bowl is full
Then I will find peace

When Buttercup snuggles close
And the day comes to an end
Then I will find peace

When a friend listens
Or a friend needs listening
Then I will find peace

When the kitchen is clean
And the laundry is folded
Then I will find peace

When the children are in bed
And His angels are all around
Then I will find peace

When the family is fed
And the dishes are done
Then I will find peace

When my kids
Are grown and happy
Then I will find peace

When I see my friends
Thrive, grow, and follow their passion
Then I will find peace (and great joy!)

Barn Doors

GOD

When others join in
To help spread the Word of the Lord
Then I will find Peace

When I name the distraction
Focus instead on goodness
Then I will find peace

When I get over my false self
Give more of my true self
Then I will find peace

When I have surrendered my desires
And replaced them with His
Then I will find peace

When Jesus returns
And I see Him face to face
Then I will find peace

When I stop controlling
And start trusting
Then I will find peace

When the night is calm
And I know He watches over
Then I will find peace

Emma Broch Stuart

When I pray
And obey
Then I will find peace

When I slow my pace
And allow His Spirit, like the wind,
To blow across my face
Then I will find peace

When I release my pride
And follow His will
Then I will find peace

When my heart is full of love
And my life shines for Him
Then I will find peace

When I pray
And stay connected
Then I will find peace

When I stop complaining
And say thank you
Then I will find peace

As the sun sets
I know I'm at peace
Because He has given me another day!

Barn Doors

HUMANITY

When more people care about more than themselves
And give a hand up to our fellow man
Then I will find peace

When the world is quiet
And all the people get along
Then there will be peace

When the music flows
And my skirt twirls in time
Then I will find peace

When the heat melts gold
And the scars ridge high
Then I will find Peace

Please
Everyone
Accept
Christ
Everlasting

You then will find true PEACE! (John 3:16-17)

Many thanks to these poets: Conda, Linda, Chrissy, Janice, Aunt Gann, Bobbi, Donna, Tammie, Emmy, Lilia, Tina, Sarah, Dawn, Sherry, Patsy, Jenjen, Ruth, Dina, Melissa, Mary Lou, and Jenn.

Peace Finds Me

First Peter 3:11 tells us to seek peace and pursue it. Psalm 29:11 says the Lord blesses us with peace. I love that peace is both found and also finds us. The previous chapter reveals poets seeking peace. But then I wondered, what does it look like when peace finds us? Here is how God answered that question:

> I journey the world
> And search it wide
> I look for peace
> On the rising tide
>
> It's never found
> In the places I look
> On mountaintop highs
> Nor deep valley brooks
>
> One thing's for sure
> As I sail on the sea

Barn Doors

Peace is not found
Rather peace finds me

———•———

There is a hymn
Of ancient days
It goes like this:
Holy be thy name

The Keeper of time
And Creator of all
Sustainer of life
Both great and small

A song can be heard
In a heart that beats
Peace is not found
Rather peace finds me

———•———

Pain rules the world
Takes me by surprise
Nothing makes sense
In the chaos of my life

Heavy with burden
Grief is my song
I stop and remember

Emma Broch Stuart

To whom I belong

How easy I forget
What it's like to be free
Peace is not found
Rather peace finds me

Mountain Transforms to Monster

There is strength in numbers. English speakers gravitate to one another when thrown into foreign cultures. I stayed close to a community of such people when I lived in France. One day, two friends and I chatted in English while shopping in Géant—a French grocery store. An elderly woman stopped us and started speaking in English. We were surprised to hear an eighty-plus-year-old French woman speaking in our mother tongue. Of course this sparked a conversation. How on earth did she learn to speak English so well?

She shared her story with us.

During World War II she and her family lived in a small French village very close to the German border. When Germans invaded her village, they refused to let the inhabitants speak French. They were to speak German or be punished. This brave woman, along with her classmates, rebelled against this imposed rule, learned English, and communicated that way.

She thanked us—three American women living in her French city—for saving France from German rule. There's something oddly uncomfortable about someone thanking your country through you personally. We humbly accepted her thanks but let her know that we hadn't even been born yet. We directed her thanks to God and told her we were going to pray for her.

Immediately, her demeanor changed. Her smile vanished. Anger clouded her eyes and sent daggers in our direction. She insisted we not pray for her. She was angry at God, angry that her father and brothers died in the war. The transition from sweet little old lady to the bundle of pure hatred before us now was shocking to witness.

There is strength in numbers.

We spent a few minutes gently ministering to this broken, hurting soul, urging her to seek God because God loved her. She refused to believe that God loved her. God had clearly shown her many years ago that He hated her, and nothing we said could change her mind. She left our conversation shaking her head, even more bitter than before. My friends and I prayed for her right there in the soda aisle.

This lady showed such resilience as a youth to be reduced to a mountain of resentment and anger over the course of her life. That mountain didn't start off as one. One grieving tear turned into another. That triggered defense mechanisms that grew a bump in her heart into a hill of bitter pain. Pain became her companion, and they grew inseparable over the decades until a mountain now sat where her heart once beat.

So many years after that day in the soda aisle, empathy for her still makes me ache, and I can almost feel the weight of those chains wrapped around her hardened heart. Time certainly does not heal wounds. Rather, if left unchecked without God, pain grows to astounding proportions. The monster it becomes can reside in the sweetest of people, showing its ugly self when provoked.

The cure, of course, is to allow God to heal those wounds caused by the pains of this world. And the sooner the better, before hill turns

Barn Doors

to mountain and mountain transforms to monster. Our suffering does not change who God is. He is the same before our pain, in our pain, and after. God will not heal a heart that won't let Him. He won't comfort a soul that refuses His comfort.

Grief, for the duration of this earth, is here to stay. We don't have to make friends with it, but through Christ, we don't have to fear it either. I encourage you—as well as myself—to allow mourning its place when it comes, but not to let it take ownership of you. Surrender to God's mighty power to heal and trust Him to carry the grief. Only He can keep the monster at bay.

The Purple Monster

His name was Bastek, and his cuteness falls perfectly after a chapter about the ugly monster. Childhood carries so many little things that amount to an enormous pile of pure sweetness. My daughter's invisible friend is one such drop of sweetness. Yes, he was purple. And he was a monster.

I can't count how many birthdays Bastek had in his short life of a year or so. Every other day, it seemed, we were lighting candles and singing "Happy Birthday" to the invisible purple monster named Bastek. How could we not? I mean, all sorts of precious looked up at me with big green eyes, begging for a birthday cake.

"Whose birthday is it this time?"

Green eyes would hesitate, thinking back to who just blew out the candles a few days before. If it was Nounours, the white bear, then she announced, "Bastek!" If we sang to Bastek the last time, then she announced, "Nounours!" Occasionally, Tigger added another stripe to his stuffed-animal life. A few times, the baby Jesus figurine from the Christmas nativity would be the guest of honor.

The entire family never failed to add candles and often put on

Barn Doors

party hats. It was worth every minute just to see teenage brothers endure "Happy Birthday" to the invisible purple monster. Golly, was that fun! Having a sister was good for them. Having a toddler sister was even better because we did things like celebrate the invisible monster's birthday. Brothers who had moved on to the likes of hip-hop music and impressing girls needed to stop and put on party hats to celebrate the little things that amounted to an enormous pile of pure sister sweetness.

One brother, big ol' thing of twenty-three years, now pesters the daylights out of his sister when he's home to visit. He'll go into her teenage room and ask where Rosie the pink elephant is. Because he needs some "Rosie hugs." Then he strangles her just to hear his sister squeal. Or puts Rosie high on a shelf so sister will nag and holler because she can't reach her elephant. If he's home and she's in school, she'll return at the end of the day to find Rosie hanging from a hook in the kitchen ceiling.

I fuss at them to stop their sibling spats. But I can't help but wonder how much of the pestering she deserves. After all, this brother had to endure birthdays for her stuffed animals and invisible purple monster when he was a teenager. Would she do the same for him? Since she's the baby of the three, I guess we'll never know. Maybe she'll do it for her nieces and nephews. What would add even more sweetness to that enormous pile is when my daughter has children and the uncles visit, to make them sing and wear party hats for a niece or nephew's invisible friends. They'll groan and say, "Not again!"

Yes, again.

Love Lines

Love quotes by famous romantics would usually follow a story title like "Love Lines." Words strung together and sent to your valentine would be another good guess. One of my favorite things about being a nonfiction author is creating catchy titles that capture the chapter's essence in fresh, fun ways that don't immediately reveal the subject. Many times I write the chapter first and the title springs up out of the contents. I love when that happens!

I was pretty set on this title first though, and you'll see why. I promise, this story contains love, and it contains lines. Now, let's see how those go together to form layers of heart poetry instead of written poetry.

A few churches sponsored a youth center for Thanksgiving this past year. I know what you're thinking—this story isn't even centered around the right holiday! Seriously? Love, romance, and valentines in the first paragraph? Where are the turkeys and cornucopias?

By the way, this is the first time as an author I've ever been able to incorporate the word *cornucopia* in my writing. That makes me love this story even more.

Back to the pumpkin pies.

Barn Doors

I rallied a few ladies from my church who I knew loved to cook, and together with my Crock-Pot of mashed potatoes, we made a small dent in the menu needed to pull off a Thanksgiving meal for fifty-plus teenagers and staff. Believe it or not, between all the churches, it came together smoothly. I tagged along with seasoned volunteers who had done this before—I follow directions very well—and I even got to serve the mashed potatoes.

Eager volunteers lined up behind tables in the gymnasium, serving spoons in hand; hungry youth lined up at the entrance, empty plates in hand. Well, there's some love lines right there. Though, these two lines are not the main love lines suggested by the title. But interesting nonetheless how they slipped in. I hadn't thought of these lines before deciding to write about this experience. The little treasures in the story are catching me by surprise too. I love when that happens!

Back to those taters.

Every precious kid who came through the line greeted us with so much appreciation. As if we weren't there to serve them food-type nourishment, but rather they were there to serve us some heart-type nourishment. Volunteers were able to fill their own plates and eat with the youth. Another lady and I ate with three young men and prayed hand in hand with them after the meal.

And then the love lines happened. The love lines that prompted my heart to share this story. Yes, the love lines directly connected to the title. *Those* love lines.

Volunteers took off plastic gloves and aprons and formed two lines at the entrance. I followed their lead. We faced one another with space in between. Those tender, grateful kids—bellies now stuffed—walked between us, full of compliments and more thank yous. Love lines connected when young men high-fived us. Love lines connected when young ladies grabbed us and held us so tightly, hungry for love and hugs. Love lines connected when one young man hesitated, hand in the air. At the last minute, he grabbed me and held on. Kid after kid walked through those two lines, they themselves forming a line.

Love flowed in gushing, torrential lines, and I couldn't hold it all. I wasn't prepared. Those seasoned volunteers did not mention this. Not one single person advised me to bring a bucket so I could collect every precious drop. No one warned me that my heart would burst from the sweetness of it all and that after the kids left, I'd be mopping puddles of myself up off the floor.

How could I have anticipated that I would walk away from this experience receiving far more than I gave? Isn't it like God, though, to write heart poetry in the most unexpected places. Only He could move in such a divine way that lines become rivers that gush. God is the biggest romantic of all time. Good grief, He loves us! He doesn't need to string words together to show us His love; He strings people together. And I never seem prepared for just how enormous His love really is.

You can be sure I'll be ready next Thanksgiving, though, when those love lines start flowing. Now I'm a seasoned volunteer, and I will prepare those who come after me to bring a bucket. They're going to need one. And a mop. Because bursting hearts cause gushing love-leaks—there really aren't enough buckets in the world for that.

- ♥ *We love because he first loved us* (1 John 4:19).
- ♥ *[God] will quiet you with His love* (Zephaniah 3:17 NKJV).
- ♥ *Love each other deeply* (1 Peter 4:8).

Barn Doors

- ♥ *And now these three remain: faith, hope, and love. But the greatest of these is love* (1 Corinthians 13:13).
- ♥ *Love never fails* (1 Corinthians 13:8).

Circle of Prayer

Gabriel pulled my hand out of my friend's with such urgency, I paused in my prayer. It only took a fleeting second to realize his desperate need to be included in our prayer circle. He meant no harm and no harm was taken. His faith warmed a path from my palm to my heart. I welcomed him into the circle with a squeeze and kept on praying.

My brother in Christ didn't give me time to put up a guard—that guard I carry around when relating with the opposite sex as a divorced Christian woman. No, I immediately loved him, blessed by his unwavering love for Jesus as he gripped my hand with so much force, shaking me as he cried *ameen* over and over while I prayed in English.

On my left, Gabriel prayed next, his heart cries to God echoed thick in Roma. Viorel—the assistant pastor of this little shanty church made of pallets—prayed next. And my friend finished up in French.

My friend and I then sat down on mismatched chairs, fanning ourselves, and allowed God's Holy Spirit to minister to us—the opposite of what we expected. We came to serve, to pray, to love.

Barn Doors

We received so much more than we gave. Sweat dripped from us as we worshiped with our Roma brothers and sisters. In the middle of that heatwave, I expected to hear woeful prayers for the living conditions they found themselves in—shacks, tents, and piles of garbage. Woeful prayers for the plans the French government had for dismantling their community of roughly 350 souls. Only praise filled that small space of holiness.

Tears flowed freely at the realization that I stood on holy ground in the middle of that shack. I stood shoulder to shoulder, heart to heart, with my homeless brothers and sisters in Christ. And I was so humbled. Humbled by their faith, by the absence of superficiality, and by how very equal we were. Naked children ran about while we sang in French and Roma. We were on our knees more than we were on our feet.

Somehow, my friend and I ended up standing before this broken group of people, singing "Amazing Grace" in English—something I have never done before in my life. We sang off key, forgot lyrics, yet we kept on going. Acceptance smiled back at us.

There was no place on earth I would have rather been than right there, my soul laid bare before these people. Before God. No place than right there, in the heat and broken humanity with my friend at my side. I am forever changed, and I know she is too.

God met us there, in that place. I didn't expect to find Him in such wretched conditions. I intended to bring Him with me and share Him with these people, being the "hands and feet" kind of Christian that I am. I'm afraid that if someone had asked during service who among us was the most broken, I would have raised my hand.

We don't find God in a building—shack or otherwise. I now see how desperately I needed to be in that prayer circle as well as in that place at that time. God had something for me, and I found it and will keep it forever. He dismantled the pitiful box in which I had placed Him. He rose above circumstance, social status, and language, and laid Himself bare. And glory of glory, He graciously allowed me to witness it, and I will remember.

Our Heart's Closet

Imagine standing at the door to a closet piled to the ceiling with clutter. Quick! Close the door before any of it falls out. What is it about stuff that gives us a sense of security? I mean, it's hard work to shove it all inside before company arrives, making sure no one sees the piles. You resolve to clean up the junk. But where do you even begin decluttering?

You realize you can't tackle this challenge on your own. You need help. Help comes armed with trash bags and cardboard boxes. Item by precious—and not so precious—item, you get that closet cleaned out, straightened up, and organized. Junk is thrown away, memorabilia is stored on clean shelves, and you sit with a cup of tea and realize that what awakens in you is better than the "safe clutter." A sense of accomplishment fills you. You learn that keeping junk just makes the job harder when you have to eventually clean it out of your closet. You breathe in the fresh air of freedom that comes from not having to hide your junk anymore. And you are refreshed at the new contents lining the shelves. Before, it embarrassed you for anyone to see your cluttered closet. Now, you show everyone who stops by, even the plumber who doesn't care whether or not your closet is clean and organized.

I liken this to standing at my heart's closet of cluttered emotions, bad relationships, emptiness, hurts, lies, toxic people, and ignorance. And mixed in with this junk are fond memories, kingdom works, godly friends and activities, hobbies, desires, and a willingness to at least peek inside the closet and look at the tangled mess, even if I'm not equipped to deal with it alone.

Several years ago, realizing I could not tackle this heart decluttering on my own, I cried out to God for help. Help arrived on the wings of knowledge and wisdom gained from participating in the Lifesprings School of Ministry[2] in Grenoble, France.

Six Saturdays—with mounds of glorious homework in between—gave me seminary-level teaching that became one of the tools God used to rid my heart of cluttered junk. I learned conflict resolution, how to build a ministry project from the ground up, and the history of women in the Church. Professors taught on spiritual warfare, studying the Bible, and people-helping skills. Every drop seeped into my heart's closet.

The school of ministry gave me assurance as I grew in my faith as well as confidence and knowledge as a follower of Christ standing in the Word of God. I learned so much about God and about myself. And God used this experience to start the decluttering process.

Most profound was discovering who I am not. Truly believing God when He says I am a new creation in Christ revealed to me that I am not defined by my past. Therefore, it grew easier to get rid of the shame that came from past mistakes, allowing God to heal me and set a new shiny vase on the shelf.

God and I tackled each item from the pile, one by one, tossing the junk and polishing off the treasures. And as I neared the end of the course, I sat back with a cup of tea, and real security poured over me. Not the fake security that comes from being filled with the wrong things. I breathed in the fresh air of freedom, my heart no longer in bondage.

Knowledge and discernment enable me to spot when something unhealthy tries to jump into my closet and clutter it up. I clean faster now and with more wisdom. When the doorbell rings, I jump up and let in the plumber. Then, I show him my closet.

Pockets of Greatness

Pride and arrogance hang heavy across this nation like a curtain of storm clouds that pound angry hail stones upon every surface. The ugly spirits of pride and arrogance tempt us to be haughty and feel as if we are above reproach. As a friend of my daughter would say, "Y'all need Jesus!"

Yes, we do. And yes, I am generalizing and stereotyping—I realize it's global, not just national—but still, the air of arrogance tends to blow from sea to shining sea across this land.

And I did not say *great* land. Just land. What makes a land great is the purest heart of its people. We can focus on the narcissism that seems to reign, or we can focus on the pockets of greatness. The air of arrogance makes my heart ache, but the whispers of greatness make my heart sing with hope. Change agents are all around—they make up those pockets of greatness that in turn make this a great land.

Let's focus our attention there and stuff our pockets full of their greatness. And let their greatness be contagious.

Barn Doors

———•———

A man gets out of prison and hitchhikes north to his home state. He doesn't get very far on the highway, and fatigue settles so heavily over him that he lays down right there on the shoulder of the highway and falls asleep. Cars whiz by, not caring if the crumpled form of humanity is even alive and breathing. Until one pickup truck slows and compassion grips the driver's heart. He refuses to join the majority, choosing instead to pick up the hitchhiker, feed him breakfast, and hand him a few bucks for a bus ticket.

America's compassion makes this land great.

———•———

A farmer wakes before the crickets finish their night song, readies his tractor, and prays over his fields before the day of harvest dawns on the eastern horizon. Integrity seats him atop the machine that will bring in the crops—crops that feed the impatient people honking at him on the rural road he must travel to reach his fields. Fields that hold the grain, grain that makes the bread, bread that the ungrateful take for granted.

America's farmers stuff our bellies with greatness.

———•———

A woman has a flat tire on the side of the road one Sunday morning. A family stops to help, the dad getting out and rolling up his Sunday best. The woman doesn't want to trouble him and says, "Sir, aren't you going to be late for church?"

"Ma'am, church isn't a building. This," he says, motioning around him, "is church." And he changes her flat tire.

America's Christ-followers spread pockets of greatness.

———•———

A police officer stops his car to help an elderly lady cross the street. Such a small gesture at the end of his shift but one he gladly embraces. After many hours protecting the streets of his city, there's nothing he'd rather do than help someone across those very streets. The little grannie takes his arm, unaware that those arms just an hour before restrained a drug dealer resisting arrest, and the hour before that held a bandage to a bleeding victim of a car accident, and the hour before that cradled a screaming infant whose mother was being whisked away by ambulance after her husband beat her up. This frail, petite thing will never know that the officer comes from a family of law enforcement and military who instilled in him a love for the thing that makes America great—her people.

America's defenders are this land's pockets of greatness.

———•———

I wish I could sit every American down like children and for every negative thing they complain about, make them list three things for which they are grateful. I can see the eyes rolling now, even hear the groans. My daughter does this after school. She's learning though, that for every bad-day item on her complaint list, she has to give me three good things that she's grateful for. Almost always, two of those three are: 1) school is finally over; and 2) lunch.

The list of greatness in this great land is endless: soup kitchens,

Barn Doors

volunteers, firemen, teachers, charities, kind neighbors, support groups, adoption, people reaching out to people. And Jesus.

Yup, *y'all need Jesus*! Let's be contagious!

"America, the Beautiful"
by Katharine Lee Bates

O beautiful for spacious skies,
For amber waves of grain,
For purple mountain majesties
Above the fruited plain!
America! America! God shed His grace on thee,
And crown thy good with brotherhood
From sea to shining sea!

O beautiful for pilgrim feet,
Whose stern impassion'd stress
A thoroughfare for freedom beat
Across the wilderness!
America! America! God mend thine ev'ry flaw,
Confirm thy soul in self-control,
Thy liberty in law!

O beautiful for heroes proved
In liberating strife,
Who more than self their country loved,
And mercy more than life!
America! America! May God thy gold refine
Till all success be nobleness,
And ev'ry gain divine!

Emma Broch Stuart

O beautiful for patriot dream
That sees beyond the years
Thine alabaster cities gleam,
Undimmed by human tears!
America! America! God shed His grace on thee,
And crown thy good with brotherhood
From sea to shining sea!

Humanity Has a Name

Thirty lime-green shirts sent a wave of color down hopeless streets in New Orleans. Thirty lime-green shirts announced our presence—well, either the thirty lime-green shirts announced our presence or the message Lord, Send Me spelled out across each one.

We were on a mission.

Lime green stood shoulder to shoulder with lime green. We fed the hungry, hugged the lonely, prayed for the weary. We cried with hurting hearts, shared Jesus with lost souls, and knocked on closed doors.

This was my first mission trip in America. My lime-green shirt carried a message louder than Lord, Send Me. The louder message was Lord, Use Me to make a lasting difference. Lord, Make Me Tender toward hurting people. Lord, Give Me Ears to hear their hearts.

Lord, Change Me from the inside out—and use this mission trip to do so. That change happened when I put a face to a name and a name to humanity. When I didn't hand a sandwich to a random stranger but rather handed it to a young man like Jaylynn, surviving by prostituting himself. That change came, not when I hugged a crying woman living in homelessness, but when I embraced LaKeisha, held her tight, and whispered a prayer in her ear. That change happened during a prayer circle on the street, hand in hand with Louisiana's humanity. When Mr. Robinson broke that circle by grabbing my hand and announcing after prayer, "I got in before the amen!"

Change came for me when I recited Psalm 19 for a man named Josh, who had tears in his eyes and was living in the park. When I watched my shy friend—wearing lime green—boldly share Jesus with Lawrence. And when Jefferson smiled and I invited him to come back to Missouri with us because our town needed a little more color. Our town needed his stories, his compassion for others who found themselves in his same situation. The world needed the beautiful smile that he carried despite his circumstances.

Knowing humanity's name changes you. When you leave their presence, you take a piece of them with you. But more importantly, you leave a piece of yourself tucked in their heart and wrapped in love. Knowing humanity's name creates a bridge between social classes that focuses on similarities instead of differences.

If only I'd had the time to sit eye to eye with every single person who made up Louisiana's nameless humanity and hear every story, engrave every name on my heart. This book would be filled with their stories instead of mine. My heart longs to go back, recognize a familiar face down the street, and call out to them by name. I would run and embrace them and say, "It's been too long!" My heart would say, "I remember you. You were not forgotten. You are remembered and prayed for by name. You are not invisible or voiceless." We would link arms and stroll down the street, talking about old times—you know, old times being just last year when God stopped life for a moment so our paths would cross and we could exchange names.

Barn Doors

When our connectedness first sprouted like the glorious flower God intended relating to be.

Their names are added here, as if etched into a wall of remembrance:

- ♥ LILLIAN ~ who questioned God's goodness because she woke up from a surgery gone bad and was missing a leg.

- ♥ JEROME ~ a beautiful black man covered in silver paint, surviving as a street artist. Posing with him and my team was a delight. He placed us in hilarious positions and was a total camera hog.

- ♥ MEGAN ~ a beautiful girl with a beautiful spirit who is too young to be living on the streets of New Orleans. But then again, is anyone ever old enough for that?

- ♥ LADY HAWK ~ a weathered, colorful woman who dabbled in all things fortune telling.

- ♥ JOSH ~ who treasured a beaded bracelet that told the story of Jesus and whose favorite book of the Bible is Psalms.

- ♥ MR. ROBINSON ~ with his contagious boldness. He surely felt the love of Christ radiating from our prayer circle and wanted in on that. He did not hesitate to jump in the middle during prayer and take my light-skinned hand in his darker one. I will never forget him or his endearing smile with one tooth that sparkled gold.

- ♥ AMARA ~ under her fortune-telling parasol, with her fragility, foreign accent, and bandaged arm, discussing the Ten Commandments.

- ♥ DAVID ~ Amara's gentle and kind friend who gave us bottles of water.

- ♥ LAWRENCE ~ living in homelessness and who made me smile because my timid friend was not intimidated by him. Even the most wretched of men need the softness of a Christ-follower reaching out in love.

- ♥ LAKEISHA ~ so tenderhearted, so touched by our generosity. We were an answer to her prayer. *Well, my love, you were an answer to my prayer.* We bonded over tears and hugs.

- ♥ JEFFERSON ~ and his warm, caring spirit for everyone living in homelessness. His guidance took us to people who were unable to come to us and our food station under the bridge. He is a guardian of humanity, a military veteran, who stuck around and helped us under the bridge. He led our team down the street to a shelter, looking back to be sure all who were under his care made it safely across the street. How he touched my heart when he leaned into the van to give me a hug and a kiss good-bye.

- ♥ THE NINE "12 DISCIPLES" ~ who nailed their oppressive names to the cross, choosing to believe the names God calls them. You are not nameless in my prayers or memories. I remember each of you. And especially Miss D, who did not just nail her oppressive name to the cross, but rather her entire life scribbled across that slip of paper.

This mission trip was never meant to throw some food and compassion at people and walk away. It was meant to connect humanity to humanity, change lives, and remember. Remember in

BARN DOORS

prayer. Remember if ever our paths cross again and I'm able to call to them by name.

I want to always remember these precious hearts who stole my heart. I want to remember them by name and celebrate who they are and what they mean to me, grateful that God brought them into my life, no matter how brief that encounter was or will ever be again.

Just Past the City Limits

Humanity isn't found just in Louisiana. It's all around, bumping elbows with us on a daily basis. The nameless of humanity hold a treasure that we only get to experience when we sit eye to eye with them. Know their names, know their stories. Humanity comes in all shapes, sizes, and colors. Hurting humanity isn't just wrapped up in poverty or exterior brokenness but can also be wrapped up in a polished outer shell with fancy shoes and a well-paying job. We don't know what folks are carrying around inside until we walk with them, know their names, know their stories.

People are God's greatest creation. They are the greatest investment of our time, compassion, and love. Many leave their mark on me and bring fondness to my heart. Like Jo who lives in West Virginia. Her daughter is a friend of mine, and I was there visiting last year. We stopped by Jo's to check on her. At ninety years old, Jo doesn't like to get out of her house very often. I imagine loneliness suffocates her at times. All of her children take turns caring for her. She spends Sunday afternoons at my friend's house.

While folding laundry the Sunday afternoon that I was there, we

Barn Doors

talked Jo into taking a drive with us so I could see the mountains in a park just past the city limits. She hesitated. You could see uncertainty cross her face. She needed to get home, stick to the routine, do nothing out of the ordinary. I encouraged her that I would love her company and also needed to see the West Virginia trees in full October fanfare before heading home.

She agreed. From the backseat, she called her other children to let them know she was "going out of town" and would be home later. As if going on an extended trip that required traveling a great distance. Going a couple of miles outside city limits was such a thing to celebrate and plan for. Just a few minutes into our travel, we crossed the city limits. She sighed from the backseat and said, "Well, I'm out of town now."

Out of respect, everyone in the car refrained from busting into loud giggles at how precious this whole adventure was. I saw "going out of town" in a fresh exciting way and wondered what else I was missing in life by doing things out of rote routine. What else did I do in my everyday life that could be paused and celebrated with zeal and excitement?

You can believe that now when I cross city limits, I often think of Jo and celebrate that I'm out of town. But it isn't just driving a car past the sign that makes you "out of town." Any time we leave our comfort zone, we are going out of town. Jo's courage to face the fear of leaving her comfort zone gave me courage to face the fears that assault me on a larger scale than driving just past the city limits.

We don't know what folks are carrying around inside until we walk with them, know their names, know their stories. Until we celebrate little victories. Until we recognize the connection humanity has with one another—big or small. One connection humanity shares is that we all deal with fear. And it feels the same for everyone. Fear is fear. And it can be crippling no matter what causes it. When we can't relate to the cause of fear in others, we can still relate to how it feels. To minimize someone else's fear—because they fear something we don't—shames them into shutting down.

Imagine if we had shamed Jo for her fear of going across city limits. She would have internalized her fear. The fear more than likely would have grown. And she would have been even more crippled by it than before.

I didn't have to understand the cause of her fear in order to relate to it. To find those treasures that all of humanity possesses, I must take care not to run everything through the filter of my mindsets, how I would react, or what a situation means to me. It isn't about me. Our trip out of town was less about me seeing the colors of a West Virginia autumn and more about celebrating Jo's victory. How blessed I am that she allowed me the opportunity to embrace going out of town in a new way—with zeal for the adventure that it brings.

Sit eye to eye with humanity. Focus on your similarities. Connect. Take a trip out of comfort zones that sends you just past the city limits. Then, by all means, pause and celebrate.

Different Streets

It happened. But we didn't stroll down the street arm in arm, joyfully remembering old times.

My church planned another mission trip to New Orleans. Prior to going, we had several mission trip meetings. I told a fellow mission-goer that I hoped to recognize someone I met last year and be able to address them by name. She said, "No, you don't. Because it would mean they are in the same situation." I accepted what she said, and even agreed, but the impact of her words did not penetrate very deeply.

Those thirty lime-green shirts returned to Louisiana. Only this year we wore blue He Rose shirts instead of Lord, Send Me. Thirty "heroes" for Jesus drove to the bridge—caravan style—while Tropical Storm Cindy slammed us with wind, rain, and tornado warnings. Stopped at a red light, I took in the city street through raindrops running down the side window of the van. Bent in the rain, a man struggled to push a red shopping cart laden with soggy belongings. A wheelchair was hooked over the cart's bottom frame, a frail woman occupying the seat. At times, the man pulled instead of pushed, rain drenching them both.

The light turned green and our caravan continued. Under the bridge, blue heroes unloaded the hot meals we had prepared, and humanity's hungry lined up to receive. That's when it happened. A friend hollered at me and asked, "Isn't that Amara?" I looked in the direction she pointed and saw the man I'd seen earlier pushing the red shopping cart. The frail woman in the wheelchair was indeed Amara, and the man was her friend David. My heart soared from recognition, then immediately plummeted when I realized how dire their circumstances had become.

I wasted no time rushing them as they made the final few feet to shelter under the bridge. David collapsed over the cart, his arms resting on the heap of dirty, wet belongings. I addressed them by name. They remembered me, and Amara wailed with hopeless tears, "I don't want to be homeless anymore!" I hugged her while David caught his breath from the long haul he'd made getting her there.

Blue heroes dished up food for them while I ministered to David. Because he remembered me, I was able to bypass all the preliminary salutations and awkwardness and encourage him with boldness. Witnessing his devotion to Amara blessed me beyond measure. And I told him so. I put my hand on his shoulder and closed my eyes. As I prayed, I felt his arm go around my shoulder, and then he pulled me closer so his head could rest against mine. His boldness brought waves of tears as I sobbed through my prayer over him.

What is it about people humbly taking what you offer that floods you with such love? The Holy Spirit enabled me to offer David something I doubt, given his circumstances, anyone else offers: recognition, affirmation, acceptance, relationship, physical touch. He reached out and touched me back, cried through the words of

Barn Doors

affirmation I poured over him, looked me in the eye and accepted my acceptance, accepted me as I accepted him—one human being loving on another human being.

We are all equal at the foot of the cross. Nothing reminded me of that more than spending those few minutes with David.

I didn't want to leave him there. Blue heroes were packing up, and anxiety nipped at me. How do you just leave? Just turn around and walk away? I couldn't. I stood there crying, telling him how much God loved him and cared for him and saw him. I told him I had prayed for him by name for an entire year and that it was hard to leave. David scooped me up in a bear hug and saturated me with the stains of his circumstances: sweat, rain, dirt, the filth and smell of homelessness. His tears.

It never entered my mind to care. I hugged him just as fiercely as he hugged me while sobbing into the crook of my neck. I didn't care because I was too busy saturating him with the stains of my circumstances. The imprints of a life lived for Jesus, marks of the Holy Spirit empowering me to share hope to the hopeless and love to the unlovable.

David's stains of circumstances washed away in the shower that afternoon. Mine on him were given with the intent to stay, cover, remain. Seeds planted, love grown. We didn't stroll down the street arm in arm, joyfully remembering old times. Maybe—hopeful, prayerful maybe—we'll stroll down the streets of heaven arm in arm. Heaven's joy transforming our "old times" into eternal, forever times.

The Ark of Waiting

For how many seasons of life could God possibly answer our prayers with "Wait"? Well, every season.

> "Lord, open the door for a new job."
> "Wait."
> "Lord, bring healing to this relationship."
> "Wait."
> "Lord, please make the suffering end."
> "Wait."
> "Lord, I long for a baby."
> "Wait."
> "Lord, loneliness is consuming me, please bring me a spouse."
> "Wait."
> "Lord, heal my body, take away this illness."
> "Wait."

I think God's favorite word is "wait." It feels that way sometimes.

Frustrations rise, hope diminishes, faith wavers. And yet God continues to say, "Wait."

Waiting brings its own sense of mourning. Mourning the thing that is no more or the thing that's just out of reach. We even cycle through several of the five stages of grief. We let anger consume us only to then bargain with God that if He will do such and such, we'll do this or that. Depression drives us into a hole of self-pity. We rise up in anger again, thinking of a new way to bargain with God.

On some levels, even the fourth stage of grief—denial—can overwhelm us. We deny that God loves us. Deny that He even hears our prayers. The hardest of the five, though, is acceptance. Accepting that God knows better than we do. Accepting that His will is for our good and He sees the big picture whereas we don't.

Prayers answered with a "no" or "wait" can do one of two things: cause us to be bitter toward God because we believe He's holding out on us or drive us to seek Him more because only He can deliver.

I speak from personal experience. I've done so much waiting, you might say I'm an expert on the topic. Waiting doesn't get easier. It just somehow changes you and your perspective—but only when the waiting is done actively instead of passively. Actively waiting puts me on my knees praying a lot, looking for little signs that God hears and sees. Passively waiting sends me into fits of whining and stomping my feet. The hardest for me is discerning if a certain matter is something God even wants me to wrestle with Him about or let go entirely. Sometimes I get "no, never" and "wait" mixed up as I listen for that little voice from the One who controls it all.

If God wants me wrestling over a longing that He has placed in me, then I can be assured there's something He wants me to learn in the process of waiting—and wrestling. As a Christ-follower who desires to walk always in obedience, I have often been overcome with guilt that I have somehow sinned in my seasons of waiting.

God poured some incredible sweetness over me while reading through the Book of Genesis. Noah's ark is such a kid-friendly story that I never expected it to touch that troubled place inside of me where guilt battled with longings and obedience warred with the stages of grief.

As I read the story of Noah in Genesis 8, the first thing to catch my eye was that twice Noah "waited seven more days" (verses 10 and 12). This may seem insignificant—it's just two weeks—but imagine being stuck inside an ark with a multitude of animals for an entire year. Two weeks of more waiting would seem like two years. Imagine the smell alone as you counted down the seconds of those fourteen days. *Frustrations rise, hope diminishes, faith wavers. And yet God continues to say, "Wait."*

Noah waited on God to tell him when to come out of the ark. I noted, however, seven things that Noah actively did while he waited:

- He opened the window
- He sent out a raven
- He sent out a dove "to see" if the water had receded
- He reached out his hand, took the dove, and brought it back to himself
- He again sent out a dove
- He sent out a dove one last time
- He removed the covering and saw dry surface

Have I been patient enough? Do I find satisfaction in God and

Barn Doors

God alone? Or have I been consumed with a particular longing He placed inside of me? This passage of Scripture has given me so much comfort and drawn me closer to God by removing the guilt element that I have somehow sinned in my waiting.

I realize from this passage just how loved I am. In my waiting and sending out doves and opening the window and even removing the covering and seeing the dry surface. The ark of waiting was never meant to be a prison or punishment. It was for preserving a remnant, for protecting that remnant. The ark of waiting was designed to carry God's purposes.

It never occurred to me that if God placed a certain longing within me, then He is waiting too. Waiting to fulfill it. Waiting for circumstances and hearts to align with His plan. God too was waiting for that dry ground so His purpose could walk off the ark of waiting and bring glory to His name.

The ark of waiting was also an ark of preparedness. A season of waiting in which to prepare for the future, for God's will to repopulate the earth. Walking righteous during that year in the ark prepared God's people for walking righteous post-ark. They depended fully on God's provision in the ark. Would they cry out to the Lord in total dependency after? Were they anxious with thoughts of what it would be like after they stepped out onto a new ground, without another human being anywhere?

Parallels run deep between the ark and Noah and the seasons of waiting we find ourselves in today. Those seasons are used to prepare us for God's purpose. God uses that time to show us what our character is made of and what comes to the surface that needs to be dealt with. The contents of the heart spill out when tested in seasons of waiting. Maybe, just maybe, there are things within you that cannot go into the next season. Maybe, just maybe, there are mindsets and giftings God needs you to have before you walk into the next season.

While we toss and turn on the waters of uncertainty and waiting, let's consider the ark of waiting as a place of protection where we gain what we need for the moment God tells us to come out and set our feet on a new ground.

Homeless for a Day

At twelve, my oldest son was like most pre-teens—selfish beyond reason. I decided he needed to be homeless for a while to realize that food didn't just magically appear in the fridge. The evening prior to our planned day of homelessness, I started my period. Oh, joy. Never one to back away from a challenge, I threw a box of tampons into my backpack while everything in me screamed to call it off. Needless to say, I went into this experience less than amused at God's timing.

Eight o'clock the next morning, we hit the streets and spent twenty-four hours roaming the park, picking up trash, and being as discrete as possible. Did I mention that we'd only been in France a few months and didn't even speak the language yet?

I journaled our experience, probing my son for his thoughts and feelings. He honestly felt like he was dying without video games and junk food. We rationed our backpack of food and water, and the only thing that kept us going all day was the thought that at 7:00 p.m. we'd make it to our rendezvous point. There—by the fire hydrant on the corner of our street—we'd find a trash bag of food that, prior to our adventure, I'd organized someone to leave for us.

Not only did the prearranged trash bag contain our supper, but the food was packaged in plastic containers—silverware and napkins were even provided. That was one of the best meals I've ever eaten. I fully expected the food to just be tossed into the bag and that we'd have to eat it with our hands.

After supper came the hardest part of our journey—settling down for a long night. By chance, we lived above a doctor's office with an underground nook that was partly covered. As I spread out my pitiful blanket, I felt a small sense of peace that just three floors above, my warm bed waited for me. That didn't comfort me enough to embrace the long night with gladness. You see, patients who waited for the doctor's office to open used the underground nook to urinate and throw their cigarettes. Not to mention the cobwebs and crawling bugs. It was the most awful, unsanitary experience of my life!

My son whined and complained, begging me to just let him race up the steps to the haven above. He'd learned his lesson. No one would know we didn't last the full twenty-four hours. *You won, Mom.* I won? What did I win? A day of using public rest rooms was *not* my idea of winning. The restlessness of staying on the move so people wouldn't know we were homeless was also not my idea of winning. Neither was rationing food, sleeping in urine, and counting every minute until this ordeal was over.

I refused to allow everything I'd endured to have been endured in vain. What was the point of doing this? Would it give my son compassion for those less fortunate? Would he be more grateful and take less things for granted? Maybe. But definitely not if I let him quit. Quitting guaranteed that he would take nothing away from this experience except more greed and a spirit of giving up and doing things half-heartedly. No, integrity would not allow me to quit one second before 8:00 a.m. the next morning.

Barn Doors

"Hunker down, big boy," I told him. "You're in for a long night."

And it was a long night. But as we sat on the steps the next morning, counting down the seconds until I could take a shower and he could raid the fridge, I knew we'd done a life-changing thing. For me, the change was immediate. For my son, I accepted that it could take a generation before it changed his life. I visualized him one day with his own self-involved child and how this experience would serve as a great reminder of the things we take for granted. I look forward to being the one to remind him.

Bathroom Buddies

Teen girls pile out of the church van—their chaperones along with them—off to see a movie about human trafficking. While in the parking lot, I give the order to pair up and find a bathroom buddy. A lot of mocking and teasing ensues as girls fake-giggle and grab the arm of a friend and skip toward the theater. "Oooh, you're my bathroom buddy!" Ha! It's all cute and funny until someone gets kidnapped. Or lost. They feel lowered to elementary age—I have just put a dent in their independence, and I don't care.

Fast forward many months to a Christian concert where 15,000 attend. Twenty-six of that massive crowd were from my church. Teens and chaperones. I was not among them. I heard about the experience later in the week. The foreign exchange student from Thailand got lost in the bathroom. She handled it very well though, texting chaperones and calling cellphones of teens she knew were seated. Thank goodness she had their numbers! She flagged down a security guard, used his phone as well. Someone finally got her text and she eventually rejoined the group.

Upon hearing the story, my first question was, "Where was your bathroom buddy?" Apparently, they were not assigned. Because the helicopter chaperone—*c'est moi*—did not go. Since this incident, we—teens as well as chaperones—have found every occasion to bring it up and joke about the need for a bathroom buddy. Even in a fast food place. Even at church.

Apparently, it's still cute and funny even after someone *does* get lost. Consider this though: there's some solid theology underneath all the bathroom buddy jokes, getting lost at an overcrowded concert, and assigning or not assigning bathroom buddies. God intended for us to do life together, never wanting us to go it alone. Even He sees the need for a bathroom buddy. They give us accountability, prevent aloneness and isolation where the enemy is more likely to harass us, and serve as a helping hand and guide to keep us from getting lost. Or help us find our way if we do get lost.

The lessons gleaned from the concept of bathroom buddies will spill over into many situations. Just the other day I used it to strengthen my point in Bible study that gals need an accountability partner for getting their homework done. I told them to partner up and get busy holding hands!

We may link arms with our bathroom buddy and joke about being too old for one, but down deep, we're glad we have them. Ecclesiastes 4 says that two are better than one because if one falls down—or gets lost—the other can help them.

Two are better than one, because they have a good return for their labor: If either of them falls down, one can help the other up. But pity anyone who falls and has no one to help them up (Ecclesiastes 4:9-10).

We were created with a gravitational pull toward community,

even if that community consists of one bathroom buddy. Of course there are times we are called to get away by ourselves. But even then, we are in community with the One who created community.

But when you pray, go into your room, close the door, and pray to your Father, who is unseen. Then your Father, who sees what is done in secret, will reward you (Matthew 6:6).

Bullets of Profoundness

None of these bullets made the cut for their own chapter in *Barn Doors*. They're too itty bitty and I couldn't stretch them long enough. But their deepness secures their place here. Profound ponderings and drops of goodness that I have gathered over the years on slips of paper, backs of napkins, texts to myself—emails too—sticky notes stuck everywhere, written on my hand, and scribbled on church bulletins. While *Barn Doors* in essence is a compilation of them, this chapter gives you the itty bitty ones in neat bullet form. That way you don't have to rummage through slips of paper, napkins, sticky notes, texts, emails, or bulletins.

- God created everything from nothing. If God creates something from something, that something was nothing before God created it.

- Just because a deer is safe in the woods at night doesn't mean I would be safe in the woods at night. What is safe for one person is not necessarily safe for another person.

When God moves you on from a circumstance, that circumstance may be well and fine and safe for others, but it is a circumstance that is no longer safe for you.

- Proof of healed insecurities is when you no longer secretly delight in the hardships and difficulties of others to build yourself up.

- One day while at the mall in Grenoble, France, I invited a couple to church. The husband responded, "My wife's Catholic and I'm a scientist." I told him scientists were welcome too. It isn't an either/or thing with God. Science and God go hand in hand because God made science.

- How you see Jesus is how you follow Jesus. If He's just fire insurance, you'll sign the document and put it in a safe in case the house burns down. (I hope you read the fine print!) If He's your truth, life, and way, then you'll trust, live, and obey.

- Parts take on meaning in light of the whole. Our testimonies evolve. Do we value just parts of it and omit others, or do we allow God to use it wholly?

- Even in the silence, there is music. Listen.

- Read this truth somewhere: "I am not afraid of storms for I am learning how to sail my ship." Profound and confirming words for me after asking God to confirm a situation and He swung those barn doors wide by using Acts 27 when

Barn Doors

Paul was a prisoner on a ship headed for Rome. A storm arose and the sailors let down the lifeboats, but Paul told them in verse 31 that they would not be saved unless they stayed on the ship. I guess if you have to stay on the ship, you may as well learn how to sail it in the storm.

- The best tablecloths are tablecloths that make a kitchen happy.

- The number right before a big number is also a big number. For example, if today is the last day you are forty-seven before you turn forty-eight tomorrow then celebrate today as the last day of being forty-seven.

- I spotted a little bird caught inside an enclosed chicken coop. In a snowstorm. A cat had also spotted the little bird and crept toward the coop. I opened the door to give the bird a means to escape. After several tries shooing it toward the door, the situation seemed hopeless, so I started to pray. The bird flew into the chicken wire and got stuck. It wiggled and wiggled then finally freed itself and flew off. I never dreamed or imagined God would answer my prayer by sending the little bird through a narrow hole in the wire. I had faith He would save the bird, but He didn't save the bird the way I thought He would. The most obvious way isn't necessarily God's way.

- The word *all* doesn't leave room for exceptions. All doesn't leave room for doubt, second-guessing, or maybes.

- Driving in the fast lane gives me heart palpitations. I never get around the semi fast enough for the SUV behind me. I'm tailgated, honked at, given the bird, and I know those flashing headlights in my rearview mirror mean Fast-laner has one hand off his steering wheel. Frightening. And then I get over in the comfy slow lane and Fast-laner passes me, giving me another horn blast for good measure. Yes, the slow lane is more my style. It promotes relationship as I allow others to merge, go at their pace, and any headlight flashing is only to signal the all-clear.

  Take away from this analogy whatever you like, but remember one thing: Driving habits reflect more about our personalities than we realize.

- Winter drags its feet from mid-January to mid-March and pulls my energy down with it. Dreary. Void of color. Breathing deep sighs of impatience doesn't make it usher spring in any faster. Driving with a friend one such dreary day, she pointed to the naked trees and said, "I love when the trees lose all their leaves. You can see the bird nests that are invisible during the spring and summer." And I realized that "void of color" was more about perception than actual color.

Now that these appear in *Barn Doors*, I can throw away those slips of paper, napkins, and church bulletins. I can take down the sticky notes, delete texts to myself—emails too—and wash the writing off my hand.

Barn Doors

Until the next profound thing strikes me and I reach into the depths of my purse and pull out a receipt I don't need. And the collection of ponderings starts all over again.

In Between

Thank you for sunsets and sunrises.
And the moonlight in between.
Thank you for rainy days, flower gardens, and for the color green.

Thank you for fresh starts and growing hearts.
And nurturing love in between.
Thank you for calm rest, a comforting embrace, and humble gifts unseen.

~ For Baby Bird because you are my in between

Bridge Between Two Camps

The majority of the time, people will fall into one of two categories. Those who like dessert and those who don't. Pro-life and pro-choice. Introverts and extroverts. Democrats and Republicans. Ford and GMC. Christian and non-Christian. Those who like the pastor and those who don't. Those who prefer rainy days and those who prefer sunny days. Chocolate and vanilla. Dog lovers and cat lovers.

It seems everything in life requires an "either/or" mentality. Either you support something or you oppose it.

As the youth group helper one Wednesday evening, I observed seventeen teens interact with one another while standing around outside. Someone in the group tattled—loudly—on a young man who wasn't present at that moment and how he was engaging in some inappropriate behavior. This group of teens immediately split into two groups—those who liked and supported the young man and those who did not.

I watched a few stragglers struggle to pick a group. They were torn between the two camps and didn't know where to go. But one thing was sure—they were uncomfortable being in the middle, and they desperately felt the need to join a group. One young straggler questioned a couple of opposers, not voicing opposition but just questioning the how and what of it all. An opposer took this young straggler by the shoulders and said, "If you keep defending him, we are going to judge you."

And the straggler shut up. The fear of being a straggler was stronger than the fear of picking the wrong side. And she joined the opposing camp. Maybe she joined the opposing camp simply because they got to her before the supporting camp did. Maybe she joined the opposing camp because the threat of being judged came from an upperclassman and she did not want to be ostracized at school. Maybe society has already impacted her young mind into believing she had to pick a side. Right then. Right there.

If only we were so desperate when it came to choosing to walk in God's light or...walk in darkness. On this battlefield, many folks struggle choosing the eternal group they want to belong in. I know some who dabble in many religions to "cover the bases." They pick every camp so they don't pick the wrong one. This is the one area where you don't want to be a lukewarm straggler.

Revelation 3:16 says, "Because you are lukewarm—neither hot nor cold—I [the Lord] am about to spit you out of my mouth!"

I don't want to be labeled supporter or opposer of this or that; Democrat or Republican; introvert or extrovert; dog lover or cat lover. I do, however, want to be known as a Christian on fire for God who refuses to straddle the lukewarm fence between holy and unholy, hoping at the last minute I can jump into the right camp. I want to know that I know that I know all the days of my life that I chose God's holy camp, even if those standing in solidarity with me number only a few compared to those standing in the opposing camp.

As far as being "either/or" in this world, you'll find me picking one of two groups in the things that matter. Like choosing hope over despair. Love over hate. Joy over misery.

Misery deceives you into believing you'll find strength in numbers. The line is drawn, and you stand on that line. Misery screams for you to cross to its side. The tiny voice of joy beckons from the other side of the line. Glimpses of a table overflowing with harvest catch your eye, and Joy stands there, waiting to serve you. ~ excerpt from *Broken Umbrellas*

Christ is the bridge between two camps. The bridge in which we can cross from misery to joy, hate to love, despair to hope. He bridged the gap between Gentile and Jew. He bridged the gap between us and God. But we are the ones who must step across the bridge.

Not only is Jesus the bridge between misery and joy, hate and love, despair and hope, He is also the bridge in whatever situation you find yourself in. Bondage from addiction, abuse, depression, or emotional turmoil? Jesus is the bridge to freedom. Whatever camp Satan has you trapped in, Jesus is the bridge to the other side.

I pray I not only cross that bridge all the days of my life but that I walk folks across so they know joy, love, and hope. I also pray my heart is guarded against ever wanting to fit into one of two worldly camps. Don't make me choose between rainy days and sunny days. And if my choices are chocolate or vanilla, give me a scoop of both.

The Attitude Jar

Attitudes stick to us like lint. We pick off the obvious ones that cling to the front of our sweaters. But what about those attitudes that sneak up on us and attach in places we can't see? It's like sitting down in the cat's favorite corner of the couch only to get up and not be aware that the back of our pants are covered in fur. We need a holy lint brush rolled over those areas to free ourselves of unseen attitudes.

The attitude jar sat outside my front door. It held the attitudes that stuck to my daughter—when she was seven—during her day at school. While walking home, I would gauge her mood and pick up on any attitudes that weren't hers but rather her classmates'. For example, my daughter did not have the spirit of ungratefulness. If she was ungrateful, she was not allowed to enter the house until she shook off that attitude into the attitude jar.

Sometimes it worked and she entered the house with giggles and a new smile. Sometimes it didn't work and she resisted giving up hurtful attitudes. Like one day when walking home, she verbally

Barn Doors

attacked me because I did not buy the "cool" after-school snacks. She treated me with disrespect and hatefulness. She pouted and dragged her feet all the way home. She stomped to her bedroom, flung herself across the bed, screaming and crying. I sat with her and prayed. She threw pillows at me. I asked her questions to which I received more hatefulness. I clearly saw her pain and that she just didn't have the right coping skills to voice that pain. I told her she needed to go back outside and visit the attitude jar. I pulled her up by the hand. She howled but followed. Throwing her head back, tears streaming down her face, she said, "I hate the attitude jar! The attitude jar isn't even real!"

Real or not, the attitude jar helped her see that the way she was acting was not okay and not of God. It gave her a concrete way to cope with the day-to-day junk that comes from relating with others. Relationships are hard, and attitudes move among us like the wind—invisible. But just like the effects of that blowing wind *are* visible, so are the effects of negative attitudes. If we as adults find it hard to lint roll the bad ones out of our lives, how do we expect our children to resist the rotten attitudes of others?

Both adults and children need to know they are loved unconditionally. They need the skills necessary to identify attitudes that are hurtful, to identify the attitudes that keep them from being spiritually healthy individuals. When we rid ourselves of wrong attitudes and replace them with positive, godly ones, the world needs a lot fewer attitude jars.

Connecting at the Well

No one likes to talk about Jesus more than I do. That's a deep well as far as I'm concerned, and if you'll sit by the well with me, that's pretty much all we'll talk about. You don't even have to sit—just get close enough to the well for a conversation and I'll talk your leg off.

I never realized how much I like talking about Jesus until I moved back to the Midwest after living in Europe for fourteen years. A few months after arriving, a missionary friend I'd met in France was passing through town and wanted to meet up for lunch. We talked about ministry, seminary, church, our testimonies—all things Jesus. After a couple of hours, as we readied to leave the restaurant, I told her how refreshing it was to have someone to talk about Jesus with. Because I hadn't found anyone yet who loved to talk about Him as much as I did. She responded with, "Well, I like to talk about recipes too." Gosh, I love her!

The first few months of culture shock and adjusting had left me empty; but I got in my car after that lunch date with my heart full to bursting. The well had overflown that day. That's what Jesus does

Barn Doors

for me. When you are a people person who needs to connect with people, and Jesus is a deep well to you, you want to connect at the well with those people.

Will you let me talk about my favorite subject here? For just a few hundred words? I promise to be brief, but it will be deep. And if Jesus isn't your favorite subject, maybe by the end of this chapter He will be. Let's spend this chapter connecting at the well with Scripture.

Hands Held High

When I started the healing journey after the brokenness of divorce back in 2009, I was so spiritually weak and broken in so many ways. I clung to a small group of women who walked with me through the fire. They surrounded me in prayer many times, lifting my hands for me because I was too weak and broken.

Moses himself, in Exodus, had a couple of fellas who held his hands up for him too.

> *When Moses' hands grew tired, they took a stone and put it under him, and he sat on it.* Aaron and Hur held his hands up—one on one side, one on the other—*so that his hands remained steady till sunset* (Exodus 17:12, emphasis added).

If you find yourself drowning in brokenness, reach out to those who will lift your hands for you until you are strong enough to do it yourself.

What Other Things?

I wonder about the things Jesus had to deal with in His earthly body during His life here on earth. John 21:25 says, "*Jesus did many other things as well. If every one of them were written down, I suppose that even the whole world would not have room for the books that would be written.*"

What were those many other things? Gosh, I want to know. Until I get to heaven and find out, I'll spend my life on earth wondering and imagining. Like, did He hold newborn babies and marvel at their little elbows? Real elbows that bend! When Jesus stepped into the Jordan to be baptized, did He picture all the microscopic things below the surface, knowing the ecosystem in full detail because He was there at its creation? I wonder if He stretched His back and bent His knees, taking in all the ways a body feels in the flesh. Did He then look skyward and say, "Good job, Dad!" Did He ever stub His toe or get an ingrown toenail? How much do you think He detested mosquitos?

I think about stuff like this. And it fascinates me!

The Quiet Sign

Parents post them on their front doors. "*Shhh! I just got the baby to sleep! Don't you dare wake her or I'll pound you!*" I wonder if God, as my heavenly Father, ever feels like that with me. Zephaniah 3:17 in the New King James Version says that God "quiets you with His love." I imagine He just gets me quieted down, and then the enemy knocks on the door. "*Shhh! Good grief, I just got the baby to sleep! Don't you dare wake her or I'll pound you!*" And God does pound Satan. He won't let the enemy wake a calm soul that He quieted with His love.

Unless Satan knocking on the door—ringing the bell even—is

part of God's plan so He gets the wonderful pleasure of quieting my soul again.

Baptizing Cats

A twenty-four-year-old student in Grenoble, France jumped into a raging river to end her life. Survival instincts kicked in and she changed her mind. A man walking across the pedestrian bridge jumped in to save her and he drowned. Another man—a brother in Christ who attended my church—jumped in and saved the girl, leaving his wife on the bridge praying the whole time.

He shared this story during church one day, and my heart ached for the man who drowned, and for the girl who will live with that for the rest of her life. Only two percent of the population in France are evangelical Christians, so there was a ninety-eight percent chance this man was not saved. God quieted my heart with the overwhelming truth that He knows what it will take to send us to our knees in repentance. Maybe the man was already saved; maybe not and this experience was the only thing that would make him cry out to his Creator. Romans 10:13 says that everyone who calls on the name of the Lord will be saved. And that gave me so much comfort. I don't know if he called on the name of the Lord, but if he was ever going to, it would have been while thrashing in the deadly waters that took his earthly life.

Fast forward three years to arriving back in the Midwest and trying to deal with culture shock in general, but also culture shock within the church. The differences were enormous! I was dealing with doubt that I was where I was supposed to be. Not that anything was wrong with the country church I found myself in. Nothing was "normal" and everything, including church, felt "off"—because

I was "off." During Sunday school one day, I wanted to share this story of the woman who was saved but not without another life perishing. The conversation was appropriate. However, I could not remember where in the Bible to find the passage about everyone who calls on the name of the Lord will be saved. So I said nothing, but all the way upstairs for church service, I chastised myself for not knowing Scripture addresses better. Add that to the doubts I was already feeling and the fact that this particular Sunday we had a guest singer and his wife. They sang some original songs, playing what I think was a banjo, but it could have just been a guitar. I sat in my pew, listening to a song about baptizing cats, and asked God if He was sure this was where He wanted me to be.

The guest singer ended a song and asked us to turn to Romans 10:13 in our Bibles. He read "Everyone who calls on the name of the Lord will be saved." Then he went back to singing songs about baptizing cats.

Since that day, I have not doubted my place.

Connecting with you at the well has refreshed me. I hope I didn't talk your leg off.

Little Dips in the Well

After connecting at the well in the last chapter, I wanted to spend this chapter taking some little dips from that well. These little dips are too small to each have their own chapter. Like drops of sweetness, they have the power to fill a bucket with their Jesus connection.

SMELLS IN THE DARK

It just so happened to be me behind the wheel in the middle of the night, driving twelve of our thirty lime-green crusaders to Louisiana. Everyone was asleep—except me, which is a good thing since I was driving. Somewhere in Mississippi the intoxicating smell of pine filled the van. It was amazing. It made me well up a little, the thought that a smell could bless me in the dark. I knew those pines were there. I did not have to see them to know. It's like that with Jesus for me. I know He's there. The signs are all around me, even if the road seems dark.

Waves of Wind

The parking lot I sat in was right beside fields of wheat. It was a windy day. And I now know when waves of wind blow across fields of wheat my heart skips a beat. My eyes can't capture the motion fast enough before the wind starts over again at the corner of a field. I never want my life so hurried or distracted that I miss the Lord doing things like that. He created the wind and seeds of grain. Then He put them together and let me witness it. That's what makes me nuts about Him.

Wrinkles, Uncovered and Smiling

A few wrinkles are just annoying. I know this because I have some. When a face carries wrinkle upon wrinkle so that it's impossible to count them, and folks don't cover them, and they smile in spite of them, that's the opposite of annoying. That's downright beautiful. A roadmap of life is evident on faces like that. I want Jesus to bring a wrinkly-faced friend into my life so I can sit and listen to their Jesus stories. Because I know they have them. I stop short of praying I'll have wrinkle upon wrinkle that carry the marks of a life well spent for Jesus. I've first gotta come to terms with the few I already have.

Those Friends of Jesus

My family and I helped a friend and her four children move out of an abusive home. Her now ex-husband would not let anyone come into the house to help her. He threw stuff outside the door for us though, and we loaded it in the car. He hated us for helping her. He

Barn Doors

knew I was a Christian. We spent a lot of time with her and her kids, surrounding them with support and love. As the following weeks brought some peace to their lives in their new place, visitations were established with the dad and children. My friend shared with me that her ex-husband continued to be nasty to her, and even said nasty things to her kids like, "I hear you've been spending time with those friends of Jesus." She apologized to me for his nastiness. I assured her there was no greater compliment than someone sarcastically calling me a friend of Jesus.

Pumping Gas

I sat in the car while a friend pumped gas. Her three children sat in the backseat. Her young son was asking me questions, curious to know how the process worked of inserting your card, lifting the handle, choosing which gas to pump. Even watching the price and stopping just in time. I explained it all to him as we watched his mama. Silence followed as he took it all in. Then a sweet, thought-filled voice said, "I think I'm ready to be a grown-up now." Me too, buddy. I think. Are we ever ready? What is that final thing that you finally get, that pushes you over the edge from child to adult? For him, knowing how to pump gas filled him with all he needed to know. When we come to Jesus, we don't sit and watch how it all works and decide if it's something we can do before declaring we're ready. It's about surrender before we're ready and growing along the way.

The Name of Jesus on a Breath

My middle son moved back to the States when he was fifteen.

His sister, brother, and I were still in France. He returned for a visit a year later, and it was the most glorious feeling for this mama bird to have all three of her babies in one place at the same time. My oldest son drove his sister and me to the airport to pick up the missing baby bird. When we all got in the car, I sat behind my oldest son, who drove, and his brother sat in the front so he could control the radio. Good grief, boy music is loud! I kept looking from my daughter beside me, to my sons in front of me. My heart was full. So full I did what any Jesus-loving, heart-filled-to-brimming person would do. With tears in my eyes, I whispered a "thank you, Jesus" under my breath. It was the faintest of an audible thank you. My oldest, driving, turned down the loud thumping music and asked, "Did you just say 'Jesus'?" What makes this remarkable is that he is not a Christian, hates when I pray over a meal, and even mocks my faith. Yes, and remarkable that he heard the name of Jesus on a breath with rap music blaring.

Fluttering Triangle

I battled tormenting dreams for several months before confiding in someone I trusted. She spoke profound words over me: When filled with the Holy Spirit, He resides in you day and night, awake and sleeping. The Holy Spirit doesn't take a break while you're dreaming.

I love the image of a dove to represent the Holy Spirit. It's as if a dove's wings are fluttering inside me as I follow Christ. A prompting or a thought from deep within creates this triangle between my head, my heart, and my soul—a triangle that "flutters." Compared to Holy Spirit flutters, my thoughts are dull and heavy.

I stopped fearing my dreams, stopped giving that ground to the enemy. I slept so much better knowing a watchman sat on the wall of my heart, just fluttering away.

Soak up Some Jesus

During that Louisiana mission trip, a group of ladies in lime-green went to a women's shelter and ministered to the residents. I gave each one a Jesus bracelet and then went through the story with them. Each bead on the bracelet represents a part of the story of Jesus from birth to resurrection. These women had been through the fire, some still going through the fire. It is my experience that the more intense the battle people have overcome, the more intensely they praise Jesus for their victory. As I said each part of the story, women repeated after me. I barely got the words "birth of a baby boy" out of my mouth before they were amening and a few hallelujahs bounced around. The entire story only takes a few seconds to say, but it seemed to take me forever because I can't talk when I'm bawling my head off. I don't know how I got through it. Those precious ladies blessed me so much. They soaked up Jesus like a sponge! You can imagine the amening and hallelujahs when we got to the cross bead and Jesus dying on the cross. They raised the roof when I got to the bead that represented Jesus risen and alive again. We wrapped it all up with a heart bead to represent why—because of His great love for us.

———•———

These little dips in the well have quenched my thirst. I hope your bucket is full.

♡ Thinking

My daughter and I enjoyed our resting days, especially if we didn't have climb up and down the mountain for errands. Resting days consist of reading, watching movies, painting toenails, and otherwise being slugs. My daughter likes to organize and make lists—just like her mama does. One morning, her resting day list contained the usual, but for some reason she decided we should also get the ball rolling for our annual Valentine's Day party (my calendar said it was September fourth). Instead of pointing out that I'd like to make it through Christmas before planning Valentine's Day, I suggested we just think about it and not really plan. She added it to the list but in eight-year-old abbreviated form:

♡ Thinking

Sometimes this little woman in training emits such innocent wisdom that I'm left awestruck and speechless. Her ♡ thinking sent a gentle breeze through my heart as I pondered God's heart thinking and some of the things my heart thinks about. My pondering sent

Barn Doors

me to the dictionary to look up *heart* and *thinking*, and I left the door open for God to speak to me through this simple act of research. Among the definitions for *heart* are: the core, the center of something, spirit, and courage. This intrigued me as I asked myself what kinds of things my core, my center, my spirit, and my courage think about. Random thoughts like how difficult it is sometimes to love others; never measuring up; being misunderstood or ignored. Thoughts of the meaning of life; how I'm going to die; will I make a difference in this world.

Then I looked up *thinking* and discovered that *to think* is a vast ocean and I've only sailed on the surface. Among the definitions are: evaluate, turn toward something or someone, consider, and expect.

Expect? What does my heart—my core, my spirit—expect? To expect means *to hope for*. My core hopes for change. Not only in myself but the world. My spirit hopes for daily refreshment and continuous filling of God's grace and love. I must return to the well often for that continuous supply of heart hope.

But how often do I sit at the well and ask the One filling me what His heart hopes for? I normally grab my ration and get on with my day, forgetting that I am made in God's image and therefore His heart must be a hopeful heart just like mine.

The purpose of this chapter is to encourage all of us, in our busyness, to pause and do some heart thinking. And then commit to filling God's valentine box with our humble, homemade valentines. After all, had it not been for His heart thinking, we wouldn't have ours.

> *So God created mankind in his own image, in the image of God he created them; male and female he created them* (Genesis 1:27).

Ruth in the Season

A casual friend I'd known earlier in my life called me one day when I was going through a season of intense pain when the walls of destruction were falling in on every side. She made the mistake of asking me how I was doing. I gave her a summary. Somewhere around explaining the fourth wall crumbling in, she needed to go and said she would call back later.

I never heard from her again. My pain frightened her. I can venture a guess and come up with many reasons why that is. She herself was in a painful season. She is a fixer by nature and there was no fixing my pain. She decided she hadn't signed up for that level of sharing since we were just casual friends.

Naomi in Ruth 1 was experiencing that intense pain where the walls of destruction fall in on every side. Residing in a foreign country because of a famine in her native land, she also mourned the death of her husband and afterward, the death of her two sons. Grief and hopelessness made her bitter with pain. Stuck with two daughters-in-law, she set out for home. One daughter-in-law returned to her mother's home at Naomi's urging, and we all know

Barn Doors

who insisted on going with Naomi. Ruth was not afraid of Naomi's pain.

> *But Ruth replied, "Don't urge me to leave you or to turn back from you. Where you go I will go, and where you stay I will stay. Your people will be my people and your God my God"* (Ruth 1:16).

I wish it had been Ruth on the other end of that phone call when I was summarizing the season of pain I'd been in. I hope that I'm a Ruth to anyone sharing their season of pain with me. *Where you go, I will go.* It makes the pain more bearable when someone sits with you in it until the season turns to one of healing.

That season for me did turn to a season of healing. It came with the help of Ruths God placed in my life who did sit with me until the turning of the seasons. I share this story to encourage you that:

- The season *will* turn. Hang in there! God will turn mourning into dancing (Psalm 31:11).
- If you aren't a Ruth, that's okay! If you desire to be a Ruth who isn't afraid of someone's pain, God will grow you into that role at the right time. Pray for that.
- If you are a Ruth, stay filled! Sitting with others in their pain can empty you. You can only give when you have something to give.

After a heavy chapter like this, we need to dance.

Morning into Dancing

Not long after I became a Christian, I was prayed over one afternoon in my women's Bible study. One lady thanked God for turning "morning" into dancing. It sounded like something straight from Scripture, so I searched the Bible, assuming it to be found in the Psalms or Isaiah. It took me a couple of months to figure out that she meant "mourning" instead of "morning."

You have turned for me my mourning into dancing (Psalm 30:11 NKJV).

I would gladly welcome the blush of stupidity if not for the incredible two months I had visualizing God turning my mornings into dancing.

Barn Doors

This morning dawned light as air
I opened my eyes, and I declared
This is a morning made for dancing!

Barefoot I danced light as air
Until the morning twirled to noon
And noon skipped by and welcomed the night.

———•———

This morning arrived with rain on the grass
I opened my eyes, excited to dance
This is a morning made for prancing!

Barefoot I pranced with the rain on the grass
Until the morning shifted to noon
And noon rained on and greeted the night.

———•———

This morning came with a heavy air
I opened my eyes, and I declared
This morning there will be no dancing.

Barefoot I shuffled through heavy air
Until the morning faded to noon
And noon crept by and cried to the night.

———•———

Emma Broch Stuart

This mourning carried me to prayer
I opened my eyes and I declared
How many mornings will there be no dancing?

Barefoot I knelt to the Lord in prayer
Until the mourning gave way to healing
And healing arrived and trusted the night.

———•———

This morning dawned with a stronger air
I opened my eyes and I declared
This mourning has turned into dancing!

Barefoot I danced with a stronger air
Until the mourning stopped at noon
And noon reached out and comforted the night.

———•———

This morning dawned bright and fair
I opened my eyes and I declared
Every morning is made for dancing!

~ for Arabella and her mommy

Fill in the Blanks

Grab your pens—this will be an interactive chapter, and your input is so valuable. When you finish filling in the blanks, post your responses on my Facebook author page. My heart wants more than anything to hear from you!

My senses have been heightened the past few months to the names of God and the verbs that follow those names. It's like my antenna goes up when I use verbs in prayer or read back over the things I write about Him or notice the verbs used in the Bible to describe Him.

These verbs, coupled with God's names, are so powerful. They leap off the page at me when I read them. They pour over me like a river when I hear them. I want to know what your favorite verbs are when attached to God's names. But first, let's read some of mine.

God *authors* life.
- I depend on Him for every breath I breathe from birth to death. There's something awe-filling about that!

Abba Father *battles* for His children.
- The first time I heard Chris Tomlin's song "Whom Shall I Fear" I was in a season of waiting. An image suddenly filled my mind of God leading an army of angels swooping across the battlefield to fight for ME! Powerful!

El Shaddai *blesses* the blessable.
- The Bible says God causes the rain to fall on the righteous and the unrighteous. That's not what I mean here by Him blessing the blessable. I believe you can resist His blessings, choosing to remain unblessable.

Yahweh *clears* agendas.
- There's nothing like surrendering your life to Him only to turn around and find He has cleared your agenda and replaced it with His own.

Elohim *colors* His world.
- Goodness, I love the seasons! It's hard to believe there are colors we have never seen.

Adonai *connects* the miles.
- 4,802 miles to be exact. That's how far it is between me and those I love and left in France when I moved back to the Midwest. God connects us, and distance vanishes when you connect at a heart level.

Jehovah *covers* with His wing.
- This carries the promise that when we are in His will,

walking obediently, we are always covered with His wing (Psalm 91:4).

God _delivers_ surrendered hearts.
- This is huge for me. When my heart is surrendered to His will for my life, I have assurance that He will deliver me from whatever threatens to ensnare me.

Abba Father _disciplines_ those who belong to Him.
- Difficult to accept but true. He disciplines (same root as "disciples" or "teaches") His children like a parent. Because He *is* our parent.

El Shaddai _empties_ us of ourselves.
- If we don't humble ourselves, He will do it for us.

Yahweh _fills_ us with Himself.
- But He only empties us of ourselves so He can then fill us with more of His Spirit.

Elohim _creates_ all things.
- Genesis 1 explains how God created the heavens and the earth. And that's a very broad image. But when I slow my mind, that image comes into focus and the wow factor blows me away. God created every blade of grass. He created wrinkles over our knuckles so our skin would stretch when we bent our fingers. God created wind. He created our tears with different properties, depending on why we are crying. Tearing up from an irritant releases antibiotics that our eyes need. Weeping tears come from

the pancreas, heart, liver, and other organs. Like I said, wow factor! Every curve and bump over the earth, every waterfall. Lightning bolts and apple seeds. It all comes from Him.

Adonai *gives* giftings.
- I love how He dishes out those giftings so that our uniqueness shines through. While I am a tad envious of those who can create colorful art, I'm not at all complaining that He gave me a love for words and the spiritual gifts of faith, empathy, and helps.

Jehovah *knows* everything.
- God knows my thoughts, fears, desires, insecurities, frustrations, and temptations, and He loves me in spite of them. He prompts me to work on them, but His love never fails in the process.

God *lines* up circumstances.
- God partners people for kingdom work. That's never more evident than when He lines up circumstances so that paths will cross.

Abba Father *speaks* every language.
- When I hear my brothers and sisters worship God in their heart language, it tenderizes a place inside of me and puts things into perspective. God isn't the God of Americans. He is the God of all nations.

El Shaddai *prompts* hearts.

Barn Doors

- This is how God most often speaks to me. He prompts me to approach someone. He brings someone to mind so I'll pray for them. Those heart promptings keep our hearts beating in time with His.

Yahweh *puts* people in our lives.
- Sometimes those people stay forever, sometimes for a season. I need discernment to know the difference.

Elohim *radiates* pure light.
- There is no darkness in Him. He radiates pure light because He is pure light. And when we are in Christ, that light shines on us and in us.

Adonai *parts* waters.
- He did it for the Israelites. Real waters. He'll do it for us when we're faced with something that seems impossible to get through. We'll not only get through, we'll cross through on dry land.

Jehovah *spreads* His protection over me.
- These images of wings and protection envelope me like a warm security blanket. Even if I'm in the middle of something so hard, and He seems so far away, I cling to His promises of protection. He won't let my feet slip (Psalm 121).

God *whispers* in ears.
- And when He does, I have God bumps (different from

goose bumps) run up and down my spine. He takes my breath away sometimes.

I incorporate these God verbs in my quiet time. God loves it when we tell Him what He already knows. It shows Him that *we* know, we believe. And we trust.

God, you <u>radiate</u> pure light that <u>pours</u> over me and <u>comforts</u> me. God, you <u>fill</u> me with your Spirit, and only by your strength am I able to obey and walk closely to you. God, you <u>speak</u> every language and <u>hear</u> every heart cry. God, you <u>author</u> life and I depend on you for every breath.

Now it's your turn! What verbs would you couple with the names of God that reflect how you see Him or how He speaks to you? Maybe there's a powerful word to describe something He's done in the past or is doing now.

God _____

Abba Father _____

El Shaddai _____

Elohim _____

Adonai _____

Jehovah _____

Yahweh _____

- <u>Abba</u> is Hebrew and means "Daddy" (*Papa* in French) in a reverent and relational sense.
- <u>El Shaddai</u> is Hebrew and the Greek translation of this

Old Testament word carries the meaning "God Almighty." (*El*: God, from *Elohim* and *Shaddai*: the Almighty) *El Shaddai* is first used in Genesis 17:1 and gives the idea of "all-sufficient" God of the Mountains.

- <u>*Elohim*</u> (ĕ·lō·hîm) is Hebrew and plural for *El* meaning God. It is first used in Genesis 1:1 describing God as "the Creator" of the heavens and the earth. He is Supreme God.
- <u>*Adonai*</u> is plural, the Hebrew word for "Lord," and suggests majesty.
- <u>*Yahweh*</u> is the Hebrew covenant name of God "I AM." It's transliteration is *YHWH*.
- <u>*Jehovah*</u> is another form of *YHWH*: God or Lord. There are several compound names of Jehovah. Here are a few:
  - *Jehovah Ra'ah* (rō·'î): "the Lord my shepherd" (Psalm 23).
  - *Jehovah Rapha* (rō·pə·'e·ḵā): "the Lord who heals" (Exodus 15:26).
  - *Jehovah Jirah* (yir·'eh): "the Lord will provide" (Genesis 22:14).

Names of God

In a self-centered world where *God* is thrown around like an empty word, I pray God is always sharpening my senses and my heart aligns with the things that come out of my mouth. I need to guard my heart from ever taking that word flippantly or casually. I never want the name of God to be meaningless or empty when I say it, think it, pray it, or write it.

Incorporating other names for God into my life keeps my heart fresh, my ears tuned, and my prayers reverent. I never want to forget that I serve and worship and obey a holy God. A righteous God who is all-powerful, all-knowing, and is everywhere at all times. God's names reveal His character and help me find that place inside myself where God doesn't just become a word, even when the world utters it in disgust or disrespect.

We mentioned several names of God in the previous chapter. Those are some of my favorites! This chapter is devoted to more names, and they come with promises attached to them. Consider them promises straight from God to you because they *are* to you. He *is* unchanging, faithful, and loving *to you* and *for you*. Of everything He created, *you* are the one He madly loved enough to send His Son to die.

Creator
"For My hand made all these things, thus all these things came into being," declares the LORD. *"But to this one I will look, to him who is humble and contrite of spirit, and who trembles at My word"* (Isaiah 66:2 NASB).

For you created my inmost being; you knit me together in my mother's womb. I praise you because I am fearfully and wonderfully made; your works are wonderful, I know that full well (Psalm 139:13-14).

Deliverer
The LORD *is my rock, my fortress and my deliverer; my God is my rock, in whom I take refuge, my shield and the horn of my salvation, my stronghold* (Psalm 18:2).

Gracious
Yet the LORD *longs to be gracious to you; therefore he will rise up to show you compassion. For the* LORD *is a God of justice. Blessed are all who wait for him!* (Isaiah 30:18).

Light
When Jesus spoke again to the people, he said, "I am the light of the world. Whoever follows me will never walk in darkness, but will have the light of life" (John 8:12).

Spirit
God, who knows the heart, showed that he accepted them by giving the Holy Spirit to them, just as he did to us (Acts 15:8).

Holy
"I am the Lord, your Holy One, Israel's Creator, your King" (Isaiah 43:15).

I am the Lord, who brought you up out of Egypt to be your God; therefore be holy, because I am holy (Leviticus 11:45).

And by that will, we have been made holy through the sacrifice of the body of Jesus Christ once for all (Hebrews 10:10).

Loving
"For God so loved the world that he gave his one and only Son, that whoever believes in him shall not perish but have eternal life" (John 3:16).

Whoever does not love does not know God, because God is love (1 John 4:8).

Faithful
Your faithfulness continues through all generations; you established the earth, and it endures (Psalm 119:90).

Unchanging
"I the LORD do not change. So you, the descendants of Jacob, are not destroyed" (Malachi 3:6).

"Every good and perfect gift is from above, coming down from the Father of the heavenly lights, who does not change like shifting shadows" (James 1:17).

Go on a treasure hunt through the Bible. I assure you there are many more names of God that reveal His character and promises to His children. If you are not His child, surrender your heart and be His child so you can claim them! Those names will sink down deep and guard you from ever being casual or flippant with the name of God. Then while the world throws the *word* God around like an empty soda can, you will be filled to bursting with all the fullness the *name* God brings to a surrendered heart.

Circle Around the Block

How many times in our lives do we leave Christ standing on a street corner and tell Him, "I'm just going to circle around the block"? He stands there waiting while we drive off. Though we fully intend to come right back, things in life have a way of taking us down one-way streets and through detours until we're so lost that the only way to find Him is to park the car and head out on foot. And there He stands; when He spots us running toward Him, He takes off in our direction.

But unlike Sandi Flower, He doesn't laugh at us when we collapse into His arms, tears streaming down our faces. Scared out of my wits I was, and my best friend found it amusing....

Sandi Flower and I took a road trip—just us girls—to the Provençe region in the south of France, a couple of hours from my home. It was the best car ride ever; we never run out of things to talk about. We found ourselves in Avignon, with the Pope's castle on our list of things to do.

After entering this charming city nestled within stone walls, it became instantly clear that we needed a map. By sheer luck, we

Barn Doors

passed a tourist office, and I slammed on my brakes at the corner. My bossy butt-ness overcame me, and I ordered my dearest friend (who I love with all my heart...remember that as you read on) to jump out of the car, race into the tourist office—I assured her someone would speak English—and meet me back on the corner.

"I'm just going to circle around the block," were my parting words to her. She hesitated only a second before jumping out. I drove off and quickly found myself lost in the city of doom. My "circle around the block" became a maze of one-way streets, detours, and red light after red light. Panic set in, and I envisioned my Sandi Flower in the same panicked state—being in a foreign country after all and not knowing a single word of French.

I screamed at God and then begged Him to forgive me, have mercy on me, and help me find her. An hour crawled by, and I finally parked the car and headed out on foot. Huffing and puffing, I was crying like a lunatic. I wiped my nose on my sleeve; I was beyond caring. My heart ached, and I nearly tripped over the fear that turned my legs to sponge cake.

And then I spotted her, glowing like an angel on the street corner. I raced toward her, my arms flailing. I screamed her name over and over. She took off in my direction and scooped me up in her arms, into her warm, best-friend embrace. I clung to her and sobbed. I thought I'd lost her forever. That fear made the relief I found in her hug so much sweeter. She smelled like heaven as I stood there drenching her hair with my tears. I told her over and over how sorry I was.

And then she released me, looked into my tear-streaked face... and laughed. While forgiveness shone in her eyes, she clearly found something amusing. Was it the dried snot on the sleeve of my coat? Could my dishevelled state have given her the giggles? I voiced my fears; she laughed them away. I cried my heart out; she wiped my tears.

Arm in arm, we headed back to the car as she told me what she found so amusing. After I said, "I'll just circle around the block," and practically shoved her out of the car, she watched the hind end of my car flying down the street and thought to herself, *I wonder if she'll be able to just circle around the block?* (European streets go every which way.) So, when I didn't show up, she knew I'd gotten lost.

I draw on this experience often as life pulls me in a thousand directions. I glance around my metaphoric car and wonder where God is. Then I remember that I left Him standing on a street corner. I slam on my brakes, come to Him in prayer, and tell Him how sorry I am. Forgiveness shines in His eyes, and while I like to think He doesn't laugh at me, maybe He does find me amusing and chuckles just a little.

Bank of the Jordan

"Get ready to cross the Jordan River into the land I am about to give to them—the Israelites".... "'Get your provisions ready. Three days from now you will cross the Jordan here to go in and take possession of the land the LORD your God is giving you for your own.'"...Early in the morning Joshua and all the Israelites set out from Shittim and went to the Jordan, where they camped before crossing over (Joshua 1:2,11; 3:1).

> Bank of the river
> Soaks in tears
> Mingles with current
> Washes away fears
>
> Bank of the river
> How many days
> Watch for a sign
> Wait for the way

Emma Broch Stuart

Bank of the river
Days turn to years
Kneel in the dirt
To drop more tears

Bank of the river
God soothes soul
Broken and weary
Battered and torn

Bank of the river
New fears start
How many years
Till waters part

Bank of the river
Lonely and deep
Promise awaits
Just out of reach

Bank of the river
Heart lay bare
Given to Giver
Offered in prayer

Bank of the river
Desire brings pain
Taken from Giver
Then given again

Barn Doors

Bank of the river
Wrestle with God
Given and taken
When waiting is hard

Bank of the river
Trust being formed
To cherish the promise
Roots deeply grown

Bank of the river
Feet now stand
Ready to enter
God's Promised Land

As soon as the priests who carried the ark reached the Jordan and their feet touched the water's edge, the water from upstream stopped flowing.... So the people crossed over opposite Jericho (Joshua 3:15-16).

Garments of Readiness

Singleness is a hard ministry to serve in. Believe me, it *is* a ministry. I'm able to serve in ways married gals can't. For example, I housesit for friends when they go on vacation—their house becoming *my* vacation. I love eating their food and seeing the sunrise from their yards. Even when I shaved my head, I'm not sure that's something easily done if married. So, I consider it an opportunity afforded me during singlehood.

Singleness is a hard ministry because, well, you're single. And you battle loneliness. It is a fantastic occasion for sharpening your character and growing dependent on God and God alone. Just when you've mastered that road, insensitive people jump out from behind the bushes and remind you of your singleness. But not always in an encouraging way that helps you embrace the ministry. No, the reminders jab and inflict mostly—hopefully—unintentional pain. I don't think folks realize how harsh they are. Like an announcement

Barn Doors

I heard at a church for a couple's day to celebrate Valentine's Day. The event coordinator said, "If you have someone, you can come."

Or a nonfiction book I read on missionaries where the author said that God "fortunately" had a mate in mind for her missionary friend. Because to stay single was *unfortunate*?

In times like this, loneliness brings me to tears. Not often and usually when there's no chocolate in the house. When God promises you the ministry of marriage, you can't help but wonder when? Or ask, "How long, O Lord?" God has promised me the ministry of marriage and I do wonder when and ask, "How long, O Lord?"

A thought buzzed through my head a few years ago during a Bible study on Ruth by Kelly Minter. She talks about Ruth's garments of mourning and how by her garments, she announced that she was not ready for anything new God had for her. I wondered at the time if I was portraying a woman in garments of mourning, making me unapproachable and therefore enabling my loneliness. Do I need to lose weight, wear makeup, get a new wardrobe, a new hairdo? Are these the "garments" needed to show the world that I am ready for what God has for me next?

This thread of thinking assaulted me for a few days. The thought of changing outward appearances did not appeal to me. I was talking to God about it alone in the car on my way to Dollar Tree. Alone time in the car with God is where He and I do a lot of our business. I can really pour out my heart and He's the only one who can hear me. I pulled into the parking lot and wiped my eyes.

Once inside, I started down the aisles to the right. I'm always aware of people around me, and this time I listened to two elderly sisters shopping together several aisles over and heading my direction. At least one of them was hard of hearing, so they spoke loudly. Their conversation blessed me so much! It was obvious they were close yet didn't get to shop together very often. One was worried about missing her bus back home. I grinned as I eavesdropped, even though I don't remember everything they discussed. Just precious banter between them, an appreciation for this or that item on the shelf, little details about each of their lives—sweet words sister to sister.

Several aisles later, we ended up cart to cart. I scooted over to allow them to pass; they took their time shuffling by. One sister followed the other, and after the other sister passed, she backed up a step and said to me, "You have such a beautiful smile." I thanked her. *Bless her elderly heart.* She took two shuffles forward only to back up again, look deeply into my eyes, and say, "I really mean it," as if to be sure I believed her. Embarrassed, I shook my head and told her, "It's not me. It has to be Jesus you see."

"I knew it!" She loudly agreed, to the entertainment of everyone within earshot. Wrinkled hands patted mine and gathered them up in a squeeze. We talked a few minutes about how walking with the Lord makes us radiant, changes our demeanor, and adds that sparkle to our eyes and smile. Exodus 34:29 says that Moses was not aware that his face was radiant after spending time with the Lord. Verse 30 tells us that Aaron and all the Israelites noticed. The world notices.

Indescribable peace flooded me. I couldn't even finish shopping. I barely made it to the car before I melted into a puddle of gratefulness for God's immediate response to my hurting heart. I've said it before and I'll say it again: Good grief, He loves us—loves me. I am already wearing all the garments I need to show the world I'm ready for what God has next for me. More importantly, I'm already wearing all the garments I need to show *God* I'm ready for what He has next for me.

The Jesus House

Being a single mother in a foreign country was a thousand levels of difficult. One thing that made it easier was where God placed us for those four years of mother and daughter doing life on their own—in a foreign country.

We rented the middle section of a three-level home with American missionaries above us and bachelors from Turkey beneath us. Other than maintenance-type conversations and polite salutations, we didn't interact much with the bachelors. We did, however, spend a lot of time with the American missionaries in the apartment above. We went to church together and were involved in some of the same ministries.

This home was located on the side of a mountain with the center of Grenoble within walking distance, though the bus at the bottom of the mountain was faster. Except on Sundays. God knew what He was doing placing us there. It was the perfect place to heal after divorce. The view of the Vercors mountain range was breathtaking in all seasons. The school was smaller and more intimate. Wisteria hung in fragrant clumps from my terrace during spring. Grapes wove their vines around the iron rods of the railing during summer. Nothing compared to eating supper on the terrace and reaching over to pick your dessert right off the vine.

We had close neighbors; house sat upon house, each having a backyard and privacy gate. This section of the city used to be the Italian district back in the day, and some of our neighbors were elderly Italians. One thing I loved about this neighborhood was the inclination they had—back in the day—toward giving their house a name. Apparently, it's a popular thing in other areas of France, not just in my Italian *quartier*.

Our house did not have a name. With names like *La Source*, *Mamou*, and *Clair Matin* already taken, ours needed something spectacular. Not that it would be official or anything, since we were just renting.

My daughter came up with the perfect name: the Jesus House. We talked about what it would be like to own the house and be able to put up an official plaque on the outside. What message would that give to passersby and neighbors, salespeople and religious door-knockers? Some would avoid that residence like a six-mile traffic jam. Others would be drawn to it as a safe haven.

Even now, six years later, it makes me pause and consider the fish emblem that some Christians put on the back of their cars and afterward engage in all kinds of ungodly driving habits. Would a plaque introducing our home as the Jesus House truly represent the people living in that home? It was and is something I strive for daily, to carry the fish or the Jesus House sign on my person, not just my vehicle or home.

Imagine a world where someone in need knocked on the door to a home with the Jesus House nailed on the outside. They were greeted by the bad attitude of a Christian who got up on the wrong side of the bed. Imagine if that stranger had a right to file charges and get a court order for the misleading sign to be taken down. Or worse, evict the tenants.

Imagine a church sign with Loving and Caring Family written in bold letters but the atmosphere of the church was the opposite of loving and caring. Imagine if the community had a right to file charges for the words to be removed. Or worse, changed to better represent the atmosphere of the church.

Scary imaginings on a human level. Scarier still when considering God's standard and how often we profoundly fail. Court orders for removal ought to shake us to the core and encourage us not only to hang the sign, but own the sign, live the sign, and wear the sign.

If you could name your house anything and carve that on a plaque for passersby to see hanging by the front door, what would that name be? Would it be a solid representation of the occupants of the home? Or maybe a goal for those occupants to aim for.

Deep Calls to Deep

Deep calls to deep
In the depths of the Sea
Crashing wave over wave
In God's rich pursuit of me

Music needs no music
In the waters of the Sea
Hitting high note after low note
God's rhythm bold and sweet

Heart aligns to heart
In the corners of the Sea
Blending beat upon beat
Love poured out from Thee
~ Psalm 42 ~ Deep Calls to Deep

Grace upon grace
In the mystery of the Sea

Barn Doors

Giving faith a stronger faith
From the start of mustard seeds

Footstep follows footstep
On the floor of the Sea
Piling stone on top of stone
Christ's foundation built in me

Truth only truth
Is the Way of the Sea
Shining Light into light
Heals the darkness evil brings
~ John 1 ~ Grace upon Grace

Everlasting to everlasting
In the heart of the Sea
Promising gift after gift
From God's hand held out to me

Children of our children
Called to dwell in the Sea
Keeping covenant with Covenant
For salvation's guarantee

Love unfailing love
In the arms of the Sea
Securing life eternal life
Through obedience deep in me
~ Psalm 103 ~ Everlasting to Everlasting

From glory to glory
By the power of the Sea
Beholding Lord of all lords
And the King of all kings

Dust formed from dust
In the breath of the Sea
Fixing image to His Image
God's face mirrored in me

Spirit joins to spirit
In the comfort of the Sea
Carrying believer after believer
To their home eternally
~ 2 Corinthians 3 ~ Glory to Glory

Deep calls to deep in the roar of your waterfalls; all your waves and breakers have swept over me (Psalm 42:7).

For of His fullness we have all received...grace upon grace (John 1:16 NASB).

But from everlasting to everlasting the LORD's love is with those who fear him, and his righteousness with their children's children—with those who keep his covenant and remember to obey his precepts (Psalm 103:17-18).

But we all, with unveiled face, beholding as in a mirror the glory of the Lord, are being transformed into the same

Barn Doors

image from glory to glory, just as by the Spirit of the Lord (2 Corinthians 3:18 NKJV).

Radical Hospitality

The international church I attended in France ministered to Roma gypsies. Near my home there was a small camp that I passed every time I walked down the mountain to catch a bus. I stopped by regularly to give them groceries or clothing. A dozen or more families lived in this particular camp, and the children would be outside the shacks playing when I walked up. They mobbed me every time, rummaging through my sacks as I walked, always saying please and thank you with dirty smiles. Usually, those few words of politeness were the only French they knew.

I let them have the sacks, but made it a point of going all the way into the camp and stopping by the "leader's" shack for a quick hello. After ministering to this camp for a year or more, I guess I earned enough trust to be invited in for coffee. There I sat, on the family bed pallet, surrounded by "tidy filth." By that I mean the shack was picked up—blankets folded, toys in a box—but with dirt floors, no running water, and a fire pit, it was filthy. The leader's wife took a cracked, stained mug, dumped out the previous user's contents, and poured heaping tablespoons—plural—of coffee into it along with hot water from the fire pit. After a few lumps of sugar, she handed it to me and told me with hand gestures to wait until the grounds settled to the bottom before drinking.

Now, I'm a coffee snob. Not only do I dislike generic brands of coffee, I also prefer my coffee weak. Several tablespoons in one mug—unfiltered—just about choked me. No amount of sugar would have helped it go down. What did help it go down was the circle of little dirty faces surrounding me. I giggled at them because they had apparently found the chocolate bars in the grocery sacks. Chocolate smudges covered any spot of skin that hadn't already been covered in dirt.

Their eyes grew big as they watched me accept this mug of hospitality from their mama. Dignity filled that shack when I bridged social barriers and accepted that mug of hospitality. And I drank it all, right down to the grounds.

Used for Mighty Things

As a student in a women's school of ministry, I researched secular magazines and their stronghold on women today. I didn't have a choice; it was a homework assignment. It meant leaving my comfort zone to pick up one of these magazines. I despise them so much and the brokenness they represent.

Topics of interest in secular magazines include fashion, gossip, horoscopes, dieting, fitness, sex, tanning, beauty products, cosmetic surgery, and stories of superficial love. During this assignment, three article titles caught my eye: "Breasts, Butt, Stomach: Put Value in Our Forms," "All the Things Men Love Us to Do to Them," and "Summer Desires: Satiny Body, Pretty Breasts, and Sexy Makeup."

As I scanned the table of contents in these magazines, sadness overwhelmed me. I thought about all the insecurities women must have who buy them. Insecurities that come from being in a bad relationship or being lonely and looking for a relationship. Insecurities from a poor self-image or abuse and neglect caused by a significant other or someone from their childhood. Insecurities that weigh them down, screaming at them that they are not good enough, will never be good enough. Screaming that they are failures as women and wives and mothers. Media and advertising count on those insecurities to sell their magazines. They capitalize on insecurities as well as create insecurities. Secular magazines are another tool Satan uses to put women in bondage. They breed idolatry and emptiness. Because let's face it, the majority of us will *never* measure up to the women these magazines portray. Fake women who are altered digitally before their fake faces, fake smiles, and fake bodies ever hit the newsstand.

Christian magazines can be just as empty. Insecurities within the body of Christ are just as real. And the Christian market plays on those as well. Are you a good enough Christian? Are you knowledgeable enough? Are you spending enough time with God? Are you doing enough for your church and community? Christian women feel like failures too, like they will never measure up, never stretch themselves and their schedules to meet ungodly standards.

These women—the enhanced fake ones, the exhausted Christian ones, all the way down to the emptiest ones—need Christ and His saving love. I can just imagine the articles that would appear in *His* magazine! "How to Feed the Multitude on a Budget." Or, "When Quiet Time Is Essential, Take a Holy Bubble Bath." Maybe, "How to Know When You Are Really Living the Life You Were Created to Live."

The goodness, richness, and amazing blessings of His magazine would not include articles on putting value in our forms, discovering what men love women to do to them, or focusing our summer desires on body, breasts, and makeup. "Heart, Mind, and Soul: Put Value Where Value Matters" would lift us up instead of tear us down with insecurities. "All the Things God Loves to Do for His People" would heal us instead of wound us. "Summer Desires: A Cool Breeze, Hand-picked Cherries, and a Good Book in the Shade of a Tree" would give us permission to just *be still.*

God's Word is His magazine. And it is filled with His mercies and grace, stories of love and redemption. Stories that encourage and fill you instead of leaving you emptier inside. Stories of romance and poetry made for singing to the heavens. Stories of real people with real problems, insecurities, and fears. Real people the writers of *His* magazine did not alter in any way. I love real people with real stories, honest people with honest struggles and pain. People I can relate to because I am just like them.

In this day and age, real people are rare treasures. True blessings from God. When we find them, we need to embrace them. When we *are* them, God uses us for mighty things.

When Our Colors Line Up and Fly

Two birds—partners in flight—appeared out of nowhere as I drove down the highway. Side-by-side, wing-to-wing, they were seconds away from impact with my windshield. Suddenly, they turned against the current and shot up and away from danger, but not before I witnessed the perfect harmony in which they did so. The perfect way their colors lined up and flew.

And it took my breath away.

> The tug and pull of a broken world
> Leaves me craving something whole
> Something deep, something more
>
> With heavy heart I journey on
> Lost in thought and on my own
>
> Until before me a sign appears

Look up, Christ says, you are more
You are deep
You are whole

Crave nothing from this broken world
Crave Me instead who makes you whole
Makes you deep
Makes you more

Spread a wing, I'll spread Mine
Side by side, up we fly
Away from danger and broken time

The world will see, they will know
When our colors line up and fly
You are more
You are deep
You are whole

Ribbons and Bows

On my knees, interceding in prayer for a friend, God gave me the most beautiful gift—an image of His mighty hand at work.

My friend faced destruction at every turn in her life. Every area was under intense attack. You could not hear her story without pieces of your heart breaking for her. Layers upon layers of heartache, pain, bondage... It sent me to my knees in *weeping* prayer for her many times.

During prayer one day, an image came to me of a huge sinkhole. I mean the thing was swallowing up entire city blocks. Imagine New York City's skyscrapers crumbling into a massive chasm that opened up beneath the city's foundation. Debris tumbled end over end into this bottomless pit. Clouds of dust rose and blocked the sun as the sinkhole consumed building after building.

An enormous arm was extended from the sky over the center of this devouring hole. Rubble continued falling in at such a speed that I could not see from the wrist down on this arm. It appeared to have no hand.

Then the debris stopped falling. The cloud lifted. And my friend was dangling from that once invisible hand. Destruction had been pouring in around her, over her—beating at her from all sides—and all the while that hand had been holding her so she did not fall in with it.

I shared this with my friend to encourage her that in the intense battle raging through every area of her life, God was holding her. The devastation she faced was not going to pull her down into that bottomless, hopeless, despairing pit. While this image was a gift for her and not me, I can't help but draw on it in times of personal battles.

When life throws us chaos, wreaks havoc, and threatens to destroy us, God holds His children in His hand. When we are tempted to believe God doesn't care because the trial is so great, even then He holds us in His hand. When we look around and see no way out and we are surely doomed to misery and destruction, we look up and there's His hand, holding us.

Isaiah 41:10 says, "Do not fear, for I am with you; do not be dismayed, for I am your God. I will strengthen you and help you; I will uphold you with my righteous right hand."

The gift of this passage—offered to my friend in the form of a beautiful image from God—is a *personal* promise straight from His hand. God's Word is alive and breathes among us, strengthens us, and gives His children hope.

God never promises that hard things won't happen, only that He will be with us when they do happen. Our circumstances do not change who God is or alter who we are as His children. I would do well to remember this when life seems to crash down around me, when devastation knocks at my door or tries to pull me into a pit of darkness. I would do well to remember where my solid ground is and to stand on that ground—stand in God's Word—and cling to the hand of His unchanging promises.

Barn Doors

Even when a chasm of hopelessness opens up beneath my feet and the enemy throws every weapon he has against me, God's righteous right hand upholds me. This truth is my solid ground. I would do well to let His truth penetrate my heart and soul and be my weapon, my safety. God's truth wraps around me like a belt when the enemy's sinkhole threatens to swallow me.

Which will I allow to consume me? A temporal, momentary threat or a promised, eternal truth?

I admit momentary threats have consumed me...*momentarily*. When that happens, God sends reminders of His eternal truth. Like He did for my friend with the gift of this image He graciously allowed me to deliver to her.

I would also do well to remember that the belt of truth is not the only weapon in the armor of God. Only the *full* armor of God makes me effective in spiritual battle.

> *Therefore put on the full armor of God, so that when the day of evil comes, you may be able to stand your ground, and after you have done everything, to stand. Stand firm then, with* the belt of truth *buckled around your waist, with* the breastplate of righteousness *in place, and with* your feet fitted with the readiness that comes from the gospel of peace. *In addition to all this, take up* the shield of faith, *with which you can extinguish all the flaming arrows of the evil one. Take* the helmet of salvation and the sword of the Spirit, *which is the word of God* (Ephesians 6:13-17, emphasis added).

And verse 18 of Ephesians 6 completes this passage with the

perfect gift. A gift wrapped with ribbons and bows and appropriate for all occasions:

> *And pray in the Spirit on all occasions with all kinds of prayers and requests. With this in mind, be alert and always keep on praying for all the Lord's people.*

Prayer: a gift I would do well to remember.

Gifts Piled High

Let the peace of Christ rule in your hearts, since as members of one body you were called to peace (Colossians 3:15).

Another time—interceding for another friend—God gave me another special gift. I treasure these images. And the God I serve, the ultimate multi-tasker, uses them not only to bless the intended receiver but me as well. And now, you too.

This friend was struggling with internal chaos. Turmoil claimed its hold over her life, her sleep, her peace. The battle came from within, and it was intense. Knowing God's promises and repeating them battled with the enemy's lies and plans to rob her of those very promises.

My heart ached for her. I battled for her in prayer. When the image came, it caught me by surprise. The sweetness of it took my breath away. The contrast between it and the sinkhole image for my friend facing destruction from every angle of life showed me that God's gifts for us are personal. He knows what we need.

God stood in front of this friend's door. Piles upon piles of gifts were stacked around Him. While I did not see God's face, I knew it was God. The gifts on the other hand I definitely saw. They were gorgeous! Colorful. Different shapes. There were so many. I didn't have time to count, though. My attention was drawn to God knocking on the door of my friend's home. He stood there holding a gift in His hand. It too was brightly wrapped. He waited for her to open the door. When she did, He held out the gift and she took it.

The gift was peace.

Philippians 4:7 says that God's peace goes beyond any human understanding. Which is why I could never stand at my friend's door and offer her this kind of peace. We cannot fully grasp it. And this incredible peace will guard our hearts as well as our minds through Christ Jesus. Only God can stand at her door and offer such an incredible gift. God knows what His children need. But did He force her to take it? Did He impose His peace upon her? No. She had to accept it from His hand and *unwrap* it. Action was required on her part.

In our faith walk, action is required on our part too. God desires relationship—Creator and created. Heart to heart. I seek His; He knows mine. He offers, I must do my part and receive. He knocks, I must open the door. He hands me His gifts, I must reach out and take them—and unwrap them.

The enemy often deceives us into believing God's gifts are for other people—better people. Perfect people. Why would the God of the universe ever bring gifts to my door? Doesn't He have better things to do, other people to bless? And yet there He stands with gobs of gifts waiting to be received. Waiting to be unwrapped.

Relationship carries a responsibility not only to receive from God but give to God. What could we possibly give the Creator of all things? What could He possibly need from us? He needs nothing

Barn Doors

from us, but He does want something from us. Our surrender. And obedience.

God doesn't need our surrender and obedience, but when we give them, He stands at our door with gifts piled high—some universal, some created uniquely for each person. He knocks and waits for us to open the door. Then He hands us just the right gift at just the right time, knowing what we need at that very moment.

God isn't handing just my friend the gift of His peace. He's handing it to you and me too. This makes my heart ponder the contents of those other gifts stacked around God. If He's passing out gifts then I want to unwrap them. Are you curious too? I was hoping you'd say yes!

The Gift of all Things

I took to the polls of Facebook to find out what others consider a gift from God. The answers blew me away! I want some of those answers—those gifts—mentioned here in this chapter. Each one deserves the spotlight—some a little spotlight in this chapter, others a bigger spotlight in the chapters that follow.

- The gift of children/family—what a precious gift to be protected and celebrated.

- The gift of life—life's every heartbeat is a reason to drop to our knees in worship of the Keeper of heartbeats.

- The gift of health—a gift often taken for granted. Until a new year rolls around and many vow resolutions that don't stick. This is one gift that requires the backup gift of God's strength.

- The gift of needs met—answered prayers where God places

the right people at the right time and provides the funds or materials for meeting a need. Amen!

- The gift of spiritual gifts—a tool God uses to bless His children and accomplish His purposes through us. Indeed a treasured gift from His hand.

- The gift of freedom—physically as well as spiritually. Physically because most of us reading *Barn Doors* live in a country where freedom was bought at a price. Spiritually because eternal freedom required a sacrifice.

- The gift of opportunities—to love others, serve others, and be all He created us to be. Not to mention opportunities to share our resources, time, and stories. Others need to hear what God has done for us.

- Many other gifts were written under that Facebook post, like: mercy, rest, seeing ourselves in the abstract, grace, dignity, Israel, faith, and discernment. It blesses me because God sees them and knows the grateful hearts of those who commented.

The gift of all things comes from the Giver of all things. I want to spend the remainder of *Barn Doors* discovering some not so obvious gifts. This by no means diminishes the power of obvious gifts like wisdom, faith, knowledge, and God's own Spirit poured out on His people. Those are covered in great detail in God's Word, blogs, inspirational quotes from others, and even in greeting cards. Stacks of obvious gifts are piled around God as He knocks on our doors. Their bright wrapping paper catches our eye like gifts under a twinkling Christmas tree. Solid reds mix with patterns of greens overlaid with golds. When God hands them to us, we must reach out and take them.

There! Behind the train of God's robe is another stack of gifts wrapped in colors we may not have ever considered. Let's unwrap those and see what else God has for us.

The Gift of Time

I want these final gift chapters to be encouraging. Nothing heavy. We'll hit the point and let it settle over us like a warm blanket. No condemnation, just love and a mug of comfort as each gift is unwrapped and considered, taken to heart and made personal. Let God speak to you. He whispers sometimes, so be still and listen.

Our timeclocks start at conception. God has already decided how many ticks and how many tocks will count down the moments of our lives. The Book of Job tells us that our days are numbered and God sets a limit beyond which no person can pass.

Genesis—the beginning—is the start of time as we know it. Passages capture moments that make up time and show God governing His gift. God's gift of time in Genesis gives us a basic structure with seasons, days, and years as well as an intricate view of what a life looks like within the confines of time.

One of my favorites from Genesis is the up close and personal account of Leah, the unloved wife of Jacob. When I wondered what to share in a chapter on the gift of time, this story instantly came to me. So grab your popcorn and we'll first open the curtains and give a summarized narrative so we're all eating from the same bowl.

Jacob wrestled with God and God changed his name from Jacob to Israel. The twelve tribes of Israel are the twelve sons/grandsons of Israel. Jacob—Israel—had twelve sons with four women. Leah and Rachel were his wives, and each of them gave their maidservant to Jacob. Rachel was the favored wife, but it is interesting to read that she died giving birth to Benjamin, her second son, and was buried "on the way to Bethlehem." On the other hand, Leah, the unloved wife, was buried in the family burial spot along with Jacob when he died, but also Abraham, Sarah, Isaac, and Rebekah.

Now that we all have our hands in the same popcorn bowl, fighting for kernels, here's my favorite part!

The end of Genesis 29 records the most amazing time journey I've ever read. Leah gives birth to her first son and names him Reuben and says in verse 32, "It is because the LORD has seen my misery. Surely my husband will love me now." This, ladies and gentlemen, is a pity party like no other when you name a child based on your misery. But she's not finished yet! Son number two is born and Leah names him Simeon and says in verse 33, "Because the LORD heard that I am not loved, he gave me this one too."

Our main character is still wallowing in self-pity when the third son is born in verse 34. "Now at last my husband will become attached to me, because I have borne him three sons." Leah names this son Levi.

Who is ready for a refill? We're gonna need more popcorn for this next verse. It's about to get as amazing as time itself. Verse 35 tells us this about son number four:

BARN DOORS

She conceived again, and when she gave birth to a son she said, "This time I will praise the LORD." So she named him Judah.

This time! Yes, "*This time* I will praise the Lord!" What a profound journey over time to get to the place where you leave self-pity in the pit where it belongs and you praise the Lord! Amen and amen again!

But wait! Let's journey forward in time to the genealogy of Christ and see something even more profound about God's gift of time.

Abraham was the father of Isaac, Isaac the father of Jacob, Jacob the father of Judah and his brothers, Judah the father of Perez (Matthew 1:2-3).

God did not use Reuben, Jacob's firstborn, to carry history's sacred line to Jesus. God did not even use Simeon or Levi. But the fourth son Leah bore and over whom she said, "This time, I will praise the Lord" did indeed carve that path all the way to Christ.

The gift of time is as untouchable as the wind. We feel time blow across our life much like we feel the wind blow across our face. But to grab a handful of it is impossible. I can't describe with definitiveness the gift of time God holds for us in His hands. Being in different seasons of our lives—with the ticks and the tocks of the past already past—makes the gift of time mean something different for each of us.

Maybe you look down at the gift held before you and covered in dandelion-yellow paper. The gift of time God holds out to me is packaged differently in earth tones of browns and greens.

They cannot look the same because they cannot be the same. My numbered days are different from your numbered days. I have passed the ticks and the tocks of my moments differently from how you have passed your moments.

Wonderment mixes with a little fear. How many ticks do you have left? How many tocks will be wasted? Have been wasted? Then you notice something similar between your gift and mine—wisps of ribbon flutter as God breathes on your gift. Wisps of ribbon flutter as God breathes on *my* gift. The Keeper of time breathes on both your time and my time.

Don't be bound in the chains of past time. Take the gift of time held out to you and start there. Let the ticks and the tocks of the past prepare you for the time remaining. It's a journey that leads to the most important element of time—eternity.

> *There is a time for everything, and a season for every activity under the heavens: a time to be born and a time to die, a time to plant and a time to uproot, a time to kill and a time to heal, a time to tear down and a time to build, a time to weep and a time to laugh, a time to mourn and a time to dance, a time to scatter stones and a time to gather them, a time to embrace and a time to refrain from embracing, a time to search and a time to give up, a time to keep and a time to throw away, a time to tear and a time to mend, a time to be silent and a time to speak, a time to love and a time to hate, a time for war and a time for peace* (Ecclesiastes 3:1-8).

~ The Keeper of time

The Gift of Breath

Let everything that has breath praise the L ORD (Psalm 150:6).

Kneel in the garden. Take a handful of earth and pause for a second. Close your eyes and ponder the incredible gift of that moment thousands of years ago when God formed man from the dust of the ground. Imagine the amazement of the first breath taken by man, heard by heaven. That first breath made possible only because God Himself breathed life into him. Babies taking their first breath at birth is as close as we can get to the wonderment that rocked heaven and earth when man inhaled and exhaled the breath of God for the first time.

Breath accompanies us every moment of life. We eat and breathe. Work and breath go together—we can't do the former without having the latter. Quick breaths are needed during laughter. We take breath into arguments where angry breaths carry angry words. Sensual breaths make lovemaking sweeter. We cry and breathe. Sleep brings deeper breaths of rest.

Life on earth doesn't happen without breath. Fight to fill lungs with air and awareness comes quickly of just how precious this gift is. From first breath to final breath, it is impossible to count the breaths in between. But God counts. As the Sustainer of life, He decides how many inhales and exhales will compose our lives between first and final.

Saint and sinner alike have no choice but to receive God's gift of breath. God's Word says He sends rain on the righteous as well as the unrighteous. Breath becomes as common and unnoticed as blinking.

If breath—common and unnoticed—is something God gives every human at birth, then why have I included it in the stack of gifts we are unwrapping? Wouldn't it be considered the fruit cake of gifts that carries no surprise, just a dull thud as we toss it aside and look for something more spectacular in God's stack?

Don't miss it. Don't overlook it. Pause and inhale. Fragile buds of baby's breath accent the bouquet of wildflowers tucked into the ribbons on this gift. Fabrics in soft blue surround the package presented to you. Lace and delicate finishings flow over the sides and move with the breeze. Kneel in the garden and receive this gift that's more precious than gold. Fill your lungs with the sweet things God allows to fragrance your life.

The remarkable gift found in the gift of breath is that God Himself bends down to listen. As He counts the breaths between first and final, He's listening for the breaths taken that honor Him. He listens because He wants to catch our breaths when they turn to gratitude and we stop wasting breaths in sin. Inhaling and exhaling the majesty of God brings Him glory. Breath pushes prayer heavenward. He gives the gracious gift of breath so that we will breathe for Him.

Because he bends down to listen, I will pray as long as I have breath! (Psalm 116:2 NLT).

The Gift of Authority

~ For Trent, because you hold the keys

Authority is a bossy kind of word. It's sassy and powerful. It runs counterproductive with the word *fear*. When we fear, we put our authority into the hands of fear, and fear rules over us instead of the other way around.

I touched on authority in the chapter "Little Dips in the Well" under *Fluttering Triangle*. Remember how tormented I was by my dreams? After several months of letting fear rule over me, I realized that the Holy Spirit doesn't sleep when I sleep. I stopped fearing my dreams and also stopped giving that ground to the enemy. That is authority. I took it back and ruled over my fear the way God intended authority to be used.

Authority is a gift Christ-followers—filled with God's very Spirit—must learn how to use. God is the Creator of authority and requires that we submit to His authority. We are not living *for* victory, we are living *from* victory. Victory is already ours; Christ took care of that when He defeated death through His sacrifice on the cross. When hearts surrender to the Authorship of the Lord, we receive by faith His authority to overcome. Overcome what exactly?

- Sin
  - *For sin shall no longer be your master, because you are not under the law, but under grace* (Romans 6:14).
  - God told Cain in Genesis 4 that sin crouches at our door. It desires to have us, but we must rule over it.
- Satan
  - *I have given you authority to trample on snakes and scorpions and to overcome all the power of the enemy; nothing will harm you* (Luke 10:19).
  - When we are in Christ, Satan cannot rule over us. *We rule over him!*
- Fear
  - *For God has not given us a spirit of fear, but of power and of love and of a sound mind* (2 Timothy 1:7 NKJV).
  - Fear is sin because we are commanded over and over not to fear. Boy, is this a hard one. It's a journey. When it creeps in like a snake, recite Luke 10:19!

Overcoming isn't the only thing authority allows us. We are given the authority to advance God's kingdom.

Then Jesus came to them and said, "All authority in heaven and on earth has been given to me. Therefore go and make disciples of all nations, baptizing them in the name of the Father and of the Son and of the Holy Spirit, and teaching them to obey everything I have commanded you. And surely I am with you always, to the very end of the age" (Matthew 28:18-20).

I imagine a gift like authority wrapped in a long rectangular box covered in plain brown paper. Its size causes God's arms to be outstretched as He holds the gift, waiting for us to stretch out our arms to receive it. We drop to our knees and surrender to the weight of it. Sliding a finger under the wrapping's edge, we give it a rip. Pieces of brown paper pile up beside us. Then we lift the lid. A rainbow of color jumps out as we move aside tissue paper to find a coat of many colors.

Breathtaking. Indescribable. We run our hands over the majesty of the garment revealed. How could a package so plain hold something so wondrous?

"Try it on," God urges.

We stand and slip our arms into the sleeves, the weight of the coat suddenly light. God adjusts the hood and ties the belt around our waist. The coat of authority envelopes us from our head to our feet and wraps around us like a circle of power. God stands back and motions for us to twirl. "Yes," He declares, "my authority looks great on you!" We swish back and forth to feel the hem brush our bare feet. Something jingles in the pocket.

Keys.

"To my kingdom," God says.

Holding them, we consider the cost of such a gift. And the responsibility. As if knowing our thoughts—because He does—God reassures us, "Not by your strength, but by my strength through you."

[Jesus] had no beauty or majesty to attract us to him,

nothing in his appearance that we should desire him (Isaiah 53:2, emphasis added).

One thing I have desired of the LORD, that will I seek: That I may dwell in the house of the LORD all the days of my life, to behold the beauty of the LORD, and to inquire in His temple (Psalm 27:4 NKJV).

"I will give you the keys of the kingdom of heaven; whatever you bind on earth will be bound in heaven, and whatever you loose on earth will be loosed in heaven" (Matthew 16:19).

I can do all this through him who gives me strength (Philippians 4:13).

"This is the word of the LORD to Zerubbabel: 'Not by might nor by power, but by my Spirit,' says the LORD Almighty" (Zechariah 4:6).

The Gift of Ownership

~ For Heather because sharing friendship ownership with you is a delight

What makes you the owner of something? Title and deed? Keys? Are those proof that the item in question truly belongs to you? Yes, for material possessions. In a human sense, producing a birth certificate will prove that you own the little person cradled in your arms.

What about taking ownership of things not seen, not cradled or touchable? Personality traits, struggles, seasons of life. Even your relationship with Jesus Christ. What makes you the owner of these things where ownership cannot be proven with title, deed, or birth certificate?

I'm all about getting rid of things our hearts own but shouldn't: bitterness, fear, anger, shame, ungodly behaviors. In the process of getting rid of sins and unhealthy feelings, ownership needs to take place. Not the kind of ownership that says it's mine and therefore okay to keep. Many people grab that and use it as a reason not to change. *That's just the way I am.* Rather, the kind of ownership where you take responsibility for the consequences of sins and unhealthy feelings. Taking ownership gives you the decision-making control it takes to load up the back of the car with these ungodly things and haul them off.

Another element to ownership is believing we own things that do not belong to us. God has often shown me lies the enemy has convinced me to pick up and own about myself. Hearts carry these lies and live as if ownership exists. We live what we believe.

False ownership sounds like this:

- I'm not good enough
- I have to be perfect
- I'm unlovable, inadequate, unwanted
- I'm not smart enough
- I have to bend to the control of others so they will like me

Don't sign your name to the deed of any of these falsehoods. There are many others, and God never intended for you to take ownership of them. The freedom you experience from owning only the things God has for you is indescribable. Yes, He wants you to own your sins and ungodly behaviors, but only because owning them leads you to confession and repentance and makes you grow.

God also wants you to take ownership of who you are. Own your quirks and uniqueness. Own your desires and preferences. Take ownership of the things that make up the you-ness of you. Your past mistakes are yours to own but only as a tool for moving forward into new ownerships.

Taking ownership the way God intended sounds like this:

Barn Doors

- This is where I am right now and I'm going to own it as I work through it
- I messed up and I own it
- I will not blame others for where I currently find myself
- I do not have to apologize when I fail to please people
- I choose today to walk in freedom from anything that weighs me down
- I refuse to believe the lies Satan has convinced me to own
- It's okay to just be me

The gift of ownership looks identical for everyone—and at the same time, looks different. Wrap your mind around the spectrum ends of that statement. Truth often comes multifaceted. In one of God's hands, the gift of ownership is the same for me and for you—owning sins, feelings, etc.; God's other hand holds the distinct gift of your ownership or my ownership—owning our unique purpose, personalities, who we are. You decide how your package is wrapped, the colors God chose for your gift and how He tied on the ribbons and bow. I won't describe that for you when He turns and takes it from His stack.

I will, however, describe mine.

Praying one day in a season of taking ownership of a lot of baggage—for the sole purpose of releasing and healing—I received a powerful image of the cross. I knelt there; Christ's blood given. I cupped my hands to catch every precious drop so it wouldn't be wasted. That was the turning point for me when I took ownership of my relationship with Jesus Christ. That moment, that image, shook me—in a good way. The gift of ownership challenged me and stretched my abilities beyond just going through the motions of being a Christian. It took me on a journey to understanding that no one can do my Christian walk for me—I must do it myself. I have to take ownership of what I do, think, say, teach, and believe.

The most powerful realization of my turning point was suddenly knowing deep in my soul that if I didn't take ownership of this relationship, nothing else mattered. Ownership of relationship with Jesus is the umbrella of all true ownership. I am not truly me without Christ because my identity and your identity—the youness of you—is found in Christ. I cannot take ownership of God's promises without Christ. I cannot have eternal life without Christ.

The gift of ownership is only a gift when it falls under the umbrella of True Ownership.

> *Then he took a cup, and when he had given thanks, he gave it to them, saying, "Drink from it, all of you. This is my blood of the covenant, which is poured out for many for the forgiveness of sins"* (Matthew 26:27-28).

The Gift of Surrender

Every gift rides on *this* gift—the gift of surrender. Every gift leads to this gift; every gift flows from this gift.

Some of my gift chapters use fun imagery to portray God as approachable and personable. (Just wait until you read about the ships!) This is not to disrespect, by any means. I don't know where you are in your journey to eternity, but how you view God is how you live—or don't live—for God. You live what you believe.

I believe God is approachable. I believe this because I *do* approach Him, and He meets me there. I believe God is personable because I can talk to Him and He speaks in return. He makes Himself approachable and personable because of His Son, Jesus Christ.

Surrender can bring to mind frightening thoughts of losing complete control or losing oneself entirely. And so we dig in our heels and eat the forbidden fruit that we think will give us complete control of our lives and make our world revolve around the great little god that we think we are.

And in some ways, this is true. We can eat the forbidden fruit, we can choose to dig in our heels and fight for control. We can be in charge of our journey to eternity. Adam and Eve chose. We too can choose who we will serve. There are only two choices.

Every person is on a journey to eternity. Eternity is real and it waits for us to take our last and final breath. Do you ever wonder what that moment of transition will be like? Going from this life to eternity? It is not a temporary moment you can experience and then return to this life in order to prepare for the permanent moment. When it happens, that's it!

This life on earth is our journey to eternity. Which side of eternity will your journey take you to—heaven or hell? Who have you chosen to serve while here on earth? That will determine whether you spend eternity in God's presence or spend eternity separated from God.

I want you in heaven with me. These gift chapters are wrapping up *Barn Doors* with a plea for your soul. If you have not already done so, open the door to Jesus. He's knocking and only He leads you to your heavenly Father. Don't skip over the following passages. Of all the passages I share in *Barn Doors*, let these be the ones you soak in.

God is:

<u>Creator</u>—*In the beginning God created the heavens and the earth* (Genesis 1:1).

"For My hand made all these things, thus all these things came into being," declares the LORD (Isaiah 66:2 NASB).

For you created my inmost being; you knit me together in my mother's womb. I praise you because I am fearfully and wonderfully made; your works are wonderful, I know that full well (Psalm 139:13-14).

Barn Doors

<u>Holy</u>—*"Holy, holy, holy is the Lord God Almighty, who was, and is, and is to come"* (Revelation 4:8).

<u>Love</u>—*"For God so loved the world that he gave his one and only Son, that whoever believes in him shall not perish but have eternal life"* (John 3:16).

Whoever does not love does not know God, because God is love (1 John 4:8).

Every human being—past, present, and future—disobeys God. From the tiniest lie or ill-thought to the biggest capital crime. This is called sin:

All have sinned and fall short of the glory of God (Romans 3:23).

Sin separates us from God:

But your iniquities have separated you from your God; your sins have hidden his face from you, so that he will not hear (Isaiah 59:2).

Sin comes with consequences:

For the wages of sin is death, but the gift of God is eternal life in Christ Jesus our Lord (Romans 6:23).

There is only one way to bridge the gap—caused by sin—between us and God:

For what I received I passed on to you as of first importance: that Christ died for our sins according to the Scriptures, that he was buried, that he was raised on the third day according to the Scriptures (1 Corinthians 15:3-4).

Jesus answered, "I am the way and the truth and the life. No one comes to the Father except through me" (John 14:6).

For there is one God and one mediator between God and mankind, the man Christ Jesus (1 Timothy 2:5).

For Christ also suffered once for sins, the righteous for the unrighteous, to bring you to God (1 Peter 3:18).

But God demonstrates his own love for us in this: While we were still sinners, Christ died for us (Romans 5:8).

A response is needed—surrender:

Here I am! I stand at the door and knock. If anyone hears my voice and opens the door, I will come in and eat with that person, and they with me (Revelation 3:20).

Yet to all who did receive him, to those who believed in his name, he gave the right to become children of God (John 1:12).

Barn Doors

If you declare with your mouth, "Jesus is Lord," and believe in your heart that God raised him from the dead, you will be saved. For it is with your heart that you believe and are justified, and it is with your mouth that you profess your faith and are saved. As Scripture says, "Anyone who believes in him will never be put to shame." For there is no difference between Jew and Gentile—the same Lord is Lord of all and richly blesses all who call on him, for, "Everyone who calls on the name of the Lord will be saved" (Romans 10:9-13).

Grace is the Ultimate Gift:

For it is by grace you have been saved, through faith—and this is not from yourselves, it is the gift of God—not by works, so that no one can boast (Ephesians 2:8-9).

Every gift chapter connects one to the other like a magnificent story that intertwines, depends on one another, and wraps around the Ultimate Gift. The gift of surrender doesn't come in a box covered with pretty paper and shiny ribbon. God's Son *is* the Gift. His arms open wider than a barn door and welcome us to the family of God when we surrender to His Lordship over our lives.

Knees will bow to Him. Every knee. Surrender will happen whether we want it to or not. It is only a gift while offered here on Earth; after, it is no longer a gift and comes with eternal punishment. Surrendering now, while on our journey to eternity, guarantees eternal life.

Wrap the gift of authority around you, fall into the arms of dependency, receive the gift of forgiveness that will forever change your perspective. The ticks and the tocks of earthly life won't last forever; the gift of breath will end.

The Gift of Perspective

Vessels of different shapes and sizes float on the surface of a lake the size of the Sea of Galilee. We are those vessels. Perspective is that enormous sea. Our little canoes drift alongside hand-hewn rafts, weathered fishing boats, and sleek sea-crafts made for high-speed sailing. The occasional kayak bobs along at a snail-like pace, its occupant resting against the oars.

Here I pause and gather the perspective needed to even consider sailing on these waters with you. They can be troubled. Let's be tender with one another.

My heart aches over humanity's brokenness. At the same time, my heart also rejoices over the brokenness I have healed from that I share in my nonfiction book *Broken Umbrellas*. Without that healing journey, my perspective would still be buried under layers of brokenness at the bottom of the sea. Every surrendered step from the very first one, revealed—and continues to reveal—a little more of God's perspective on humanity's suffering and brokenness. My brokenness. I don't know if I could have grasped even the tiniest hint of God's perspective had I not first suffered deep brokenness.

Maybe I would have. I will leave that wave of unknown to someone better equipped and more seasoned.

I can only take you where my compass has taken me and share stories of others who have sailed over those waters in their battered vessels. I don't know where you are on that lake—anchored to shore, fishing in the middle, or racing down its watery length. Maybe you're the kayak bobbing along at a snail-like pace while resting against the oars. My intent is not to harm you, so please hear my heart if my words don't come out right.

Suffering and struggles create rough waves; our vessels toss and rock in those choppy waters. Storm clouds conceal the moonlight that we would otherwise use to navigate safely to shore. Nothing can be trusted from the perspective of the storm. Neither compass direction nor wind direction. Neither gut feelings nor advice from fellow sailors. There we are, "straining at the oars." Lightning flashes, thunder pounds, violent waves send seawater over the sides of our sinking boats. We throw down the oars and scoop it out by the bucketful, desperate to stay afloat. More gushes in to replace what we just bucketed out. We alternate between oars and bucket. Bucket and oars.

Hopelessness pulls us down like weighted chains. Fight or flight kicks in, because let's face it, the threat of survival is real. If we put down the bucket, the boat will sink. We just know it; that is our perspective. *I have to keep scooping.* But we also need to use the oars or we'll never reach shore. *I have to keep rowing.* Oars and bucket; bucket and oars. Doing the same thing over and over, expecting different results. More gushes in to replace what we just bucketed out. Oaring takes us in circles. Vessels come alongside and offer assistance. *I have to keep scooping, I have to keep rowing.* When storm waters rage at our feet, thunder claps overhead, and winds bend us as if in a hurricane, we don't even know where we are or if we're going the right direction.

It doesn't matter if our compass is broken or the wind drives at us from all directions. We only need to glance up for a split second to see Jesus walking on the water toward our boat. If we keep scooping and don't cry out to Him, He will walk right by. He doesn't force Himself into anyone's vessel.

If we embrace the storm's perspective, then deep suffering and struggles have the capacity to harm us in greater ways than the original suffering or struggle. Joseph shows us this in Genesis when he tells his brothers who sold him into slavery that what they intended for harm, God used for good. That story would have had a completely different outcome had Joseph not clung to the arms of God. Joseph's perspective changed.

Often, during my journey to healing, I would say, "I can't imagine anyone going through what I'm going through without Jesus in their boat." There is suffering with hope of healing. And then there is suffering with no hope. *That* is what breaks my heart. Of all the suffering this world can throw at us, hopelessness is by far more painful than the suffering itself. I pray you know that deep in your soul.

I have friends who thank God for the change in perspective cancer brought to their lives. What the enemy meant for evil, God turned around for His glory. These friends steered their battered vessels over rough waters while resting in the arms of Jesus who *calmed them* with His love rather than calming the storm. He does calm storms, but mostly He calms us while in the storm.

How can shore seekers—Christ followers—praise God with their vessels tossing violently on stormy waters? Because the storm never changes the fact that the shore exists even when we can't see it.

Once we surrender to the navigational expertise of Jesus—whose compass is never broken—He takes an oar and paddles our vessels with us. Then we are never alone, never without hope. We still sail the waters of suffering and struggles because those trials produce perseverance needed to be mature enough sailors to keep aiming for shore.

It's difficult to imagine where the gift is in all this. While anchored, Jesus tells us from which side of the boat to cast our fishing nets. Gift after gift is pulled forth from the sea. Every time we cast our nets, we haul in more gifts. The gift of perspective removes hardness of hearts. Our nets catch wisdom and knowledge—*fruits de la mer*—that nourish us so we grow. The gift of perspective reveals God's unchanging character and draws us closer to Him with each piece of ourselves that we surrender. The gift of perspective offers us faith.

And faith anchors us to Hope.

Later that night, the boat was in the middle of the lake, and he was alone on land. He saw the disciples straining at the oars, *because the wind was against them. Shortly before dawn he went out to them, walking on the lake.* He was about to pass by them, *but when they saw him walking on the lake, they thought he was a ghost. They cried out, because they all saw him and were terrified. Immediately he spoke to them and said, "Take courage! It is I. Don't be afraid." Then he climbed into the boat with them, and the wind died down* (Mark 6:47-51, emphasis added).

Early in the morning, Jesus stood on the shore, but the disciples did not realize that it was Jesus. He called out to them, "Friends, haven't you any fish?" "No," they answered. He said, "Throw your net on the right side of the boat and you will find some." When they did, they were unable to haul the net in because of the large number of fish (John 21:4-6).

The Gift of Joy in All Circumstances

Impossible gifts. I accept that I'm a writer of impossible gifts. And this is one that I dragged my feet on writing. Balance is hard when you try to incorporate some personal experience with biblical passages. Too preachy or not enough? Too personal or too vague? Let me be the first to encourage you—none of these gifts are impossible. Including the one before you. It most certainly is possible to have joy in all circumstances. Joy is not just a feeling, therefore it is obtainable even in the direst of circumstances.

Joy is not the same as happiness. Happiness starts externally and travels inward. Joy starts internally and gushes outward, splashing on those in the vicinity. Think about happy things outside of yourself and how good those feel settling into the heart where memories are stored. Happiness comes; happiness goes. It is dependent on experiences exterior of you.

Joy is the opposite. It arrives on the four winds of heaven and knocks on the door of your heart. You can shut the door—lock it even—or invite joy in to stay. Another option is to let joy in and decide later if you want to grab it by the scruff of the neck and toss it to the curb. Joy comes; joy goes. But it is not dependent on experiences exterior to you. It depends entirely upon God; and He is trustworthy. He is the Keeper of promises. Joy is eternal and supersedes temporary worldly happiness.

Nehemiah 8:10 says, "the joy of the Lord is your strength." Joy comes from God. As the Giver of joy, He means for it to be lasting. When we read in Hebrews that "for the joy set before Him, Jesus endured the cross," it makes James 1:2 a little more powerful that we are told to have joy in trials.

> *And let us run with perseverance the race marked out for us, fixing our eyes on Jesus, the pioneer and perfecter of faith. For the joy set before him he endured the cross, scorning its shame, and sat down at the right hand of the throne of God. Consider him who endured such opposition from sinners, so that you will not grow weary and lose heart* (Hebrews 12:1-3).

> *Consider it pure joy, my brothers and sisters, whenever you face trials of many kinds, because you know that the testing of your faith produces perseverance* (James 1:2-3).

I struggle finding joy in all circumstances. That's why I dragged my feet writing this chapter. I'm inadequate as your guide because I don't have anything bubbly and uplifting to share. This is one area we'll have to walk hand in hand and discover together. I'm drinking coffee out of my Joy cup today. Maybe that will help.

Apostle Paul, the author of Philippians 4, writes about being content in all circumstances. Paul is my hero; I want to be like

Paul. I'd like to believe if my circumstances went from one to the other and back again, I'd eventually be able to say I'm content in all circumstances. Life throws me new trials, scary circumstances that I've never experienced before. Joy gets buried, and I can't say I'm content with them.

But I want to be. And so I focus on my favorite joy passage. "Restore to me the joy of your salvation and grant me a willing spirit, to sustain me" (Psalm 51:12).

The gift of joy in all circumstances comes wrapped in *joyful* paper with flashy zigzag colors of electric blue, eccentric purple, emerald green. Confetti flies when God gives the package a little shake. He fiddles with the card attached on top. It's one of those that play music when you open it. We've all bumped into joyful people who rub against us when we're in no mood for joy and would rather wallow in our misery. It irks us. Watching God sway to the music and toss confetti, we now know where those folks get it. We roll our eyes and pace. This is not an easy gift to accept. We ask ourselves, "Why?" It's joy, for goodness sake. That should be the easiest and most delightful gift of the entire stack. Yet we resist it, comfortable with our moodiness.

The blast of a party horn snaps us from our internal monologue. Oh great! Rejoicers have gathered and God is passing out party favors. He catches our eye, shakes the gift at us like a tambourine—confetti splashes on everyone in the vicinity—and motions for us to join in.

The gift of joy in all circumstances waits to shower us with loving confetti. Do we stand back and watch others rejoice in the gift, or do we jump under the gushing stream and let joy drench us?

The Lord takes delight in his people (Psalm 149:4).

BARN DOORS

Rejoice always, pray continually, give thanks in all circumstances; for this is God's will for you in Christ Jesus (1 Thessalonians 5:16-18).

[The LORD your God] will rejoice over you with singing (Zephaniah 3:17 NKJV).

The Gift of Forgiveness

A strand of God's love runs through these ending chapters on gifts. That strand connects each one; they go hand in hand as if in a circle that cannot be broken—the thread holds them too tightly. Start with this circle of gifts strung together with binding knots of pure love. My prayer is that as you close *Barn Doors* on these final chapters, you consider other gifts not covered here. Widen that circle and embrace them! If every good and perfect gift is from God, then the list of gifts is endless and all-encompassing. Widen the perception of what a gift from God truly looks like.

Christian duty lies at the human understanding of forgiveness. As a Christian, I must forgive if I want God to forgive me. Some offenses are easy to forgive. Others seem impossible to forgive. I don't want this chapter to be a repeat of words you've had pounded into you all your life. I'd rather embrace forgiveness as a gift and look at it with new insight.

Opportunities to forgive are presented to us daily. Your child breaks your favorite vase and says he's sorry. Friends run late for a dinner date and apologize when they finally arrive. These are but two examples of hundreds of occasions for "I'm sorry" to be said and these words to follow:

"That's okay."

My daughter went on a youth trip last summer. It was discovered on the ride home that another teen girl had stolen my daughter's money. They were in separate vehicles, and this teen's parents called me to ask if they could hang on to the money to confront their child and have her return it later in the week with a proper apology. I was actually relieved that I had that time with my daughter to prepare her for what forgiveness looked like.

Forgiveness isn't saying, "that's okay." Because it's not okay. When people do things wrong and it affects us, it is not okay. Ever.

I knew my daughter's first response to this girl would be "that's okay," because she'd just be happy to have the money back. We explored over the days before the apology why saying this was the wrong response. We explored why saying, "I forgive you," is a better response. It acknowledges that wrong was done, it shows a decision to forgive, and it offers grace. Much needed grace.

Can we say, "I forgive you," if we sincerely have not arrived at the place of authentic lasting forgiveness? I think so. Can we say, "I forgive you," even when someone isn't sorry? I think so. One definition of *forgiveness* is "the willingness to forgive." My daughter was able to say to this girl, "I forgive you," and mean it.

If only the wrongs people commit against us were as petty as stealing our lunch money. If only slander were as easy to forgive— or abuse, malicious acts, and other sins. In these cases, it takes a deep intentional decision to forgive. Our initial response may not be "I forgive you," but the journey to forgiveness in a very hurtful incident can result in a response like "I choose to forgive you in this moment, knowing I will have to make that choice again later today." And that decision to forgive gets easier the next time. Then easier the time after that.

It's the journey we often fail to realize is involved in forgiveness of deep hurts done to us. The journey isn't even possible without God's supernatural strength working through us, carrying us when we can't even put one unforgiving foot in front of the other. Showing us what forgiveness looks like.

My go-to passage in times like this is the story in Mark 9 of the father who brought his demon-possessed son before Jesus and said in verse 22, "If you can do anything, take pity on us and help us." In verse 23, Jesus countered that with, "If you can? Everything is possible for one who believes." This father's immediate response appears in verse 24 and is my go-to passage. "I do believe; help me overcome my unbelief!"

Lord, I forgive; help me overcome my unforgiveness!

This is a hard gift to grasp. It was one of the hardest to write about. Nonetheless, we watch God choose from that pile of gifts, all the while saying to ourselves, *pick the little one on top, pick the little one on top.* Of course, He bends down and chooses the biggest package of all. Snow white, the purest white, nearly blinds us as the gift is brought front and center. Threads of crimson run down the length of the Gift, circle underneath and come back around the width of the Gift to form a cross on top. It had to be the biggest gift in the stack; it couldn't be the little one on top—easy to snatch from God's hand, easy to grab and apply.

As soon as we step forward, open our arms to receive, and simultaneously confess sin from a surrendered heart, God gathers us in His arms and the Gift is crushed between us. Does God say, "That's okay"? No, because sin is never okay. Instead, He whispers, "I forgive you."

The Gift of Dependency

Dependency on anything earthly is bondage. It truly is that simple in principle, though difficult when lived out. Oppressive, earthly dependency comes from many sources, each with their own chains of bondage.

- As women, to depend on men for our identity sets us up for deep oppression that wraps chain after chain around our hearts. The same goes the other direction too. Men and women must find their identity in Christ if they want to live in freedom.

- Dependency on a substance like alcohol or drugs creates a pit of despair that eats at a person until there's nothing left but the broken pieces of a life completely given over to the compromise that comes with the next drink, the next high.

- Dependency on ANY human being for our happiness is

complete and debilitating bondage. For both the one dependent and the one suffocating because of it.

- Dependency on chance or luck makes a person lose touch with reality. They are not free to live. Their bondage insists that they focus on the next lottery drawing, the next slot machine, the next mortgage to pay off gambling debts. The "here and now" flashes by as they live in the oppression of "just wait until..."
- Dependency on our own strength to overcome any bondage is a futile endeavor.

Warm, dependable hands hold the gift. It waits, suspended in the air between God and you. Watch the way iridescent waves of deep orange shimmer when God inches the package in your direction. He won't force you to take it. Consider how the ribbon dangles in glittery curlicues from the gift itself, waiting for fingers to pull on it and release the surprise inside. The surprise is this: Dependency on God is a gift.

We fail to see sometimes that getting rid of a destructive dependency requires latching onto a trustworthy dependency. True healing from an oppressive dependency never happens without replacing it with God's gift.

It's there waiting, suspended in the air between God and you. Reach out. It's yours!

Trust in the LORD with all your heart and lean not on your own understanding; in all your ways submit to him, and he will make your paths straight (Proverbs 3:5-6).

Barn Doors

Don't you know that when you offer yourselves to someone as obedient slaves, you are slaves of the one you obey—whether you are slaves to sin, which leads to death, or to obedience, which leads to righteousness? (Romans 6:16).

The Gift of Ships

This is not an easy place to sit—on the final gift chapter. These are my last few hundred words with you, and I want to make them count. A profoundness washed over me as I proofread *Barn Doors* up to this point. It's all relational. My stories, my life. Even sitting here alone writing for you, I'm relating to you by sharing so much of myself. Even when I'm alone, praying and communing with God, it is relational. He is relational.

Amazing that in addition to creating everything—as if that weren't enough!—He created us with the ability to relate. I can't wrap my mind around a world where relating is absent from existence. Indeed, we've been given a powerful gift.

The gift of ships sails through *Barn Doors*' table of contents and anchors perfectly here, collecting it all into a treasure chest of friend*ship*, fellow*ship*, partner*ship*, and relation*ship*.

God captains the four ships; we are His sailors in our little rowboats. Who better to teach us to sail than the Captain—and Creator—of the four ships? The world is full of people sailing their ships against the orders of the Captain. Fighting for their place on

Barn Doors

the ocean of life, forgetting that it's God's ocean. I'm betting that you, like me, have people in your life where the ships aren't sailing so smoothly.

The brokenness surrounding us makes it impossible to sail perfectly. Relation*ships* and friend*ships* are strained. Fellow*ship* bitter or nonexistent. Which makes the *ship* of partnering in ministry impossible. Brokenness is a suffocating fog that keeps us from navigating with expertise. We do our best, yet we still hurt one another, disappoint, and fail to meet expectations. If only everyone else would sail the way we sail, right? Then the ocean of life would be so much smoother. We forget that every other sailor on these waters thinks the same thing.

The Captain cups His hands and hollers, "Follow me!" Then He shows us how to sail the four ships, and yet we still hit a choppy wave that throws us into other vessels. "Hey, watch out!" they say. We fuss and fume, "Can't you see I'm trying to follow the Captain?" Tensions mount, hurtful words are thrown over the starboard side, and we lose sight of the Captain.

Before we know it, we're shipwrecked. Our broken vessels litter the coastline, and we stand on the beach shading our eyes, looking to the horizon for a sign of hope. We give up. Sailing the four ships was difficult while on the water. Shipwrecked, they are impossible. The perilous situation creates the perfect environment for hostility. Every time we turn around, so-and-so is right under our feet trying to execute his or her own survival tactics. We're attempting to build a shelter with branches from a palm tree; they're building a fire in a pit. The flames shoot up and onto our roof and there goes our shelter. Our safety. They refused to sail the way we sail, and now by golly, they refuse to be shipwrecked and broken the way we are shipwrecked and broken.

Misery overtakes the castaways. Shelters are in flames, attitudes along with them. Spirits sink with the realization that nightfall is moments away. If being in shipwrecked proximity to these broken people wasn't bad enough in the daylight, spending a dark night would prove unbearable. What could be worse?

It starts to rain. *What could be worse?* Huddling with all of them for warmth and protection under the one remaining shelter, that's what. No one sleeps, either because the rain continues most of the night or because tempers—ugly and sharp—prevent sleep from arriving.

Morning dawns soggy and dismal. Circumstances remain precarious until someone spots a vessel on the horizon. Castaways stand shoulder to shoulder and watch a ship larger than life heading straight for the shores of the island.

The massive thing lowers its anchor, and God leans over the side, waves, and shouts "Ahoy, mateys!" Once on shore, He listens to us empty our hearts of the bitterness that grew while deserted with no hope on the horizon, fearing we'd be shipwrecked in our circumstances, with these horrible people, forever.

With tenderness, God asks, "Why didn't you use My gift?"

Surely He doesn't mean the gift of the ships? We already established that they are difficult when on the water, impossible to sail if shipwrecked and broken.

But God created them to be sailed whether on land or sea, and He tells us so. They were created to be sailed whether we like our fellow sailors or not. Every single one of us has access to His map—the Bible—to help us navigate. The Captain has not only revealed how to sail the four ships but also provided guidelines for certain circumstances when we should *not* sail the four ships. We truly need

Barn Doors

to access the map daily. The more we read and follow, the wiser He makes us—and the wiser He makes us, the better we sail.

Spiritually healthy people sail the four ships in a way that invites others onboard. We were created to sail the four ships. Only by following God through His Son are we able to do so well.

God takes off down the beach, and we follow Him. Our Rescuer stops, takes three paces to the right, knocks on a coconut tree, and takes five more paces straight ahead. Kneeling down, He starts digging. We join Him, sand flying over our shoulders. Before long, we reach something solid.

Buried treasure. God lifts out the chest and brushes the sand from it. Jewels sparkle in the sunlight, exquisite and breathtaking. The significance of the moment hits us all at once: We had to be shipwrecked *together* to find the treasure. We all start talking at once, only bitterness doesn't bubble up out of our hearts but rather repentance and deep appreciation for the gift of the ships: friend*ship*, fellow*ship*, partner*ship*, relation*ship*.

God turns the key in the lock while we all catch our breath with bated anticipation. The lid creaks open. Trinkets of dazzling treasure pour out upon the warm sand, waiting for grateful souls to collect its splendor and feel the weight of its worth settle deep inside where treasure is kept. Before we take the trinkets spilled out for us, we focus on our Guide. Hearts—in harmony with hearts—worship the One who captains all the ships with His mighty ship.

> *The things that come out of a person's mouth come from the heart* (Matthew 15:18).

> *Above all else, guard your heart, for everything you do flows from it* (Proverbs 4:23).

Closing Doors

Here we are, the final chapter. I'm missing our time together already! It was silly of me to think I'd be completely finished with this tidy journal before starting another collection of those scraps of paper, sticky notes, texts, and emails to myself, along with church bulletins. Alas, a few have already formed a pile, and I haven't even started the editing phase of *Barn Doors*! Does God ever stop speaking to us or showing us His goodness?

I'll leave you with two scraps of paper, knowing that later today God will reveal Himself to me in wonderful ways that will end up doodled all over the back of a church bulletin. There is no end to His love or how He shows it. And I am ready, pen in hand.

- Whatever God uses to draw you closer to Him is a gift. Grab the whatever!
- Pierre, my brother in Christ, says (and I jotted it down!) "You must live in the present, enriched by the past, while looking forward to the hope of the future."

Barn Doors

God isn't closing these barn doors; the chapter title only implies that the book is closing. It's time for you to grab a church bulletin and scribble all over the white spaces and around the edges. Listen to the whispers God gives you and jot them down. Watch for your own barn doors to swing wide. Start collecting the drops of goodness in your life as acknowledgement to the Giver of that goodness. Share your stories and insight. The world needs God to swing barn doors wide—and He can use you to do it.

The Lord *will send a blessing on your barns and on everything you put your hand to* (Deuteronomy 28:8, emphasis added).

Love You

Instead of a Thank You page, I've decided that *Barn Doors* needs a Love You page. Y'all don't mind reading through some valentines, do ya? (*Barn Doors* Fun Fact: I finished the final chapter on Valentine's Day 2017!)

Little Love—*Buttercups are yellow, Lovebugs are blue, you're mama's Baby Flower, and Sweetness pours from you.* I love you for telling me that rainbows are circles, not arcs. I love you for loving candy. I love you for loving knowledge and loving Jesus. I love you because you embrace the you-ness of you. I love you to the moon and back.

Father of Baby Wind—*Winter is white, the wind is true, you're mama's strong tower, and Jesus loves you.* I love you for holding

Barn Doors

the most memories with me. I love you for your dedication and perseverance in doing this thing called life! I love you for being a source of strength and at the same time a warm soft marshmallow.

Stain Hater—*Birds are red, oatmeal is blue, you're mama's between one, and I love you.* The middle Christmas tree that represents you—in my set of three—has a little red bird on top. His tail wing is broken, but how symbolic and sweet is that? You will always be mama's baby bird. Fly back to the nest often so I can watch you swoop in and make the perfect landing—on both feet.

Valentines galore spread out among these pages. God swings barn doors wide to reveal:
  shore seekers and a birthday buddy,
  mourners and peace finders,
  friends and a key holder,
  smokers and sock folders,
  crumb droppers and the invisible purple monster,
  stain haters and Well dippers,
  a coffee maker and heart thinkers,
  broken humanity and little old ladies,
  bathroom buddies and house namers,
  prayer partners and camp dwellers,
  hug givers and lime-green wearers,
  love collectors and boat rowers,
  wrinkled smilers and joyful rejoicers,
  scientists and fast-laners,
  relationship owners and truth searchers.

Barn Doors is my valentine to God, from first word to final. I want Him to know that when He speaks, I listen.

Notes

1. Gary Chapman, *The Five Love Languages: How to Express Heartfelt Commitment to Your Mate* (Northfield Publishing, 1992, 1995, 2004).

2. Lifesprings School of Ministry, Grenoble, France, 2010-2011, adapted from the WomenSchool of Ministry Leadership founded by Pamela H. Heim, established with Lifesprings School of Ministry's founding president Anna Pavey and led by Janice Gutierrez, Dean and current Executive Director of Lifesprings Women's Ministries International.

Also by Emma Broch Stuart

Join author Emma Broch Stuart as she travels that snowy road of pain toward the ultimate healing only God can offer.

www.ingramcontent.com/pod-product-compliance
Lightning Source LLC
Chambersburg PA
CBHW011343090426
42743CB00019B/3426